Chronicles of a

CRUISE SHIP
CREW MEMBER

Answers to All the Questions Every Passenger Wants to Ask

Third Edition

by Joshua Kinser

This book is dedicated to all of the completely insane crew members, cruise directors, staff captains, musicians, and passengers I have met and worked with through the years. Without you, this book definitely would not be as funny and entertaining as it is. So, thank you for providing so much great material.

It is dedicated to all of the cruise ship crew members of the world. Without you, these cruise ships would never leave port, and if they tried they would sink. All that hard work does not go unnoticed and unappreciated. The cruise ship companies should be paying you way more than they do.

It is especially dedicated to all of the extremely talented and fun musicians I have had the pleasure to play music with on the cruise ships over the years. This one's for all you show band guys.

A portion of the author's proceeds will be donated to Mercy Ships, a global charity that has operated hospital ships in developing nations since 1978.

Mercy Ships brings hope and healing to the forgotten poor by mobilizing people and resources worldwide, and serving all people without regard for race, gender, or religion. Mercy Ships programs promote health and well-being by serving the urgent surgical needs of the forgotten poor and empowering developing communities. Since its founding, Mercy Ships has performed more than 1.7 million services valued at over $670 million and impacting more than 1.9 million people as direct beneficiaries.

For more information on Mercy Ships, visit their website at www.mercyships.org.

Introduction   1

1 What Time is the Midnight Buffet?   7

2 How Do You Get a Job on a Cruise Ship?   15

3 What Is It Like to Work on a Cruise Ship?   25

4 What Is the Crew Area Like?   56

5 What Is It Like to Work as a Musician on a   87
   Cruise Ship?

6 Why Are All the Officers Italian?   117

7 OK. What Is It Like to Work as a Musician in   131
   the Orchestra on a Cruise Ship?

8 What Is the Worst Part About Working on a   157
   Cruise Ship?

9 What Is the Best Part About Working on a   194
   Cruise Ship?

10 Why Would Anyone Ever Stop Working on a   212
   Cruise Ship?

   About The Author   250

"Twenty years from now you will be more disappointed by the things that you didn't do than by the ones you did do. So throw off the bowlines. Sail away from the safe harbor. Catch the trade winds in your sails. Explore. Dream. Discover." - Mark Twain

INTRODUCTION

I never expected to find myself out at sea, unless that Mississippi River rafting trip I always wanted to take went way wrong. Somehow, I ended up working on cruise ships for more than five years. It was the wildest time I have ever had. For someone who is absolutely addicted and entirely obsessed with traveling, there is no better job than working on a cruise ship. As a travel writer working for magazines and guidebooks, and as a musician in touring bands and on cruise ships, I have been able to travel all over the world. I can honestly say without a doubt that a cruise ship is one of the most fascinating places you can visit. However, a cruise ship is more than just a ship. It is a city. As crew members, we are living aboard these floating cities that charge through the sea and rope up at port after port, beach after beach, and paradise after paradise. And just like cities, cruise ships have their own unique language, culture, personalities, their own bright side and even their own dark side as well. It is immensely interesting.

When crew members go out to sea and choose to work on a cruise ship, they aren't only working on the ship. Crew members are living on that cruise ship, spending most of their time in the crew areas beneath the water line that often are as fascinating as they are crowded. In this book, I would like to take you on a tour of a crew member's life and show you what it's *really* like behind the scenes aboard one these massive, metal, party ships.

A cruise ship definitely is an interesting place to live, and people (landlubbers especially) seem to harbor a curious fascination with the sea and those who venture into its waters—a fascination that will live on forever. There is a reason that people today are still mesmerized by the *Titanic*. And if you choose to go and work on a cruise ship, taking a job out at sea will naturally stir up the curiosity of those around you. From the time you set foot on a cruise ship, your life will never be the same again. For starters, it will be a life filled with questions about what it is like to work on a cruise ship. Your friends, family, and even complete strangers will want to know what you experienced out at sea. Even on my first day as a cruise ship crew member, passengers wanted to know the inside scoop. Everyone wants to know what happens down in the crew areas.

I wrote this book to answer all of these questions once and for all. However, allow me to give you fair warning before our story at sea begins. While it is easy to romanticize about what it must be like to live on a cruise ship from the comfort of your favorite armchair, believe me, working on a cruise ship is definitely not all frozen daiquiris and midnight buffets. I wrote this book about what it is *really* like to live and work aboard a cruise ship. So, this book does steer away from idealizing the ship. This book tells the complete story. And this means that the book is going to describe both the positive and negative sides of ship life. Some people may be surprised to learn that many crew members have a deep love-hate relationship with the cruise ship, but it's true. I will explore this complex experience. I will explore all of the luxurious and incredible parts of working on a cruise ship, but I will also reveal the obnoxious, nearly intolerable, and downright grimy aspects of ship life as well. Some of you may not want to read about the negative aspects of cruise ships. So, this may not be the book for you if you want to read a book that takes place in a fantasy land where all of the Filipino cabin stewards on a cruise ship are happy, smiling crew members who burp butterflies, fart rainbows, and make towel animals solely because they love to see passengers smile. And you should probably move on if you are a cruise ship employee or a veteran cruiser who would be upset by a story that makes a cruise director look like a complete boob. However, if you want to hear both sides of the story, the positive *and* the negative, then keep reading.

I am sure that some crew members may disagree with what I have written. They may disagree with my perspective of the ship. But I am equally sure that most crew members will be able to read this book, nod their heads, and say, "This is exactly what it is like."

However, I can only draw from my own experiences, and so I can only tell this story from my perspective. Yet, no two crew members are going to have the same experience. In fact, no two cruise ships are alike. This is because every ship has a different captain. Every crew member has a different attitude. Each cruise line has different rules for their employees, a differing approach to ship design, and a different style of management. There are also different crew members on every ship. A crew member can return to a cruise ship they worked on just a year earlier to find that the ship is nothing like the one they remember. And most importantly, there are hundreds of different jobs on a cruise ship, and a crew member's job will largely define what kind of experience they have. I worked on cruise ships as a musician in the lounge bands, jazz trios, and orchestras. My experience was undoubtedly very different than that of an officer working on the bridge, a cabin steward in housekeeping, or an engineer in the engine room. Yet, we all experience ship life together— the same wonderful experiences as well as those miserable aspects too.

No matter how you feel about what I have said in this book, I sincerely do hope that you find the book entertaining and one that you enjoy. I see my experience on the cruise ship through a comedic lens, and so I hope you are able to read the book with this in mind. This is a book that I am certain will leave you with a deep sense of what it is really like to work on a cruise ship. It will show you that working on a cruise ship is a lot like sailing in rough seas; there are a lot of ups and downs. And after you read this book, I guarantee that you will never be able to hear the deep and thundering sound of a cruise ship's horn the same way again. Now, let's untie this vessel from the safety of the dock and see what adventures lie ahead.

- Joshua Kinser
September 7, 2012

1

WHAT TIME IS THE MIDNIGHT BUFFET?

About two weeks is the breaking point. At least that's when I hit my breaking point on my first contract. Let me explain. There are 200 or more cruise liners that are floating out at sea right now. On each of these cruise ships there are 2,000 passengers, on average. This means that at any given moment, there are more than 400,000 passengers wandering around lido decks, standing in the hot sun waiting for a lifeboat drill to start, or searching for the next buffet. And there is one thing every crew member learns very quickly on a cruise ship; every passenger has potential—potential to ask a crew member a stupid question. And most passengers absolutely live up to this potential.

Sometimes, it is the repetition of the questions more than the fact that they are painfully idiotic that drive crew members over the edge. These questions can often be enough to send crew members heading straight for a gallant leap over the rails of the ship and into the dark blue waters below. In those cold waters, crew members will at least find bliss in the certainty that there will be no passengers, and certainly no one asking stupid questions.

Questions like, "What time is the midnight buffet?"

"Is there an elevator that goes to the front of the ship?"

"Where's my cabin?"

"What do you do with the ice sculptures once they've melted?"

"Why can't I drink alcohol at the emergency boat drill?"

"Do I have to go to the mandatory boat drill?"

"Does this ship generate its own power?"

"Do the crew members sleep on board?"

When crew members are asked their first idiotic question, they usually stop in mid-stride as they are walking down the promenade and wonder whether they have made the right decision to go work on the seven seas. Crew members will question whether *they* are in fact the idiot. The idea to get a job on a cruise ship sure sounded great when they first visited the cruise ship recruiter's office. The recruiter made it sound like crew members do nothing but get paid to sail around the world and visit sunny beaches across the globe. The recruiter made working on a cruise ship sound more fun than an eternal ride on Space Mountain at Disneyworld.

I hit my breaking point about two weeks into my first contract. I'm pushing a cart, one similar to the luggage carts you find in a hotel lobby, and it's loaded down with a poorly balanced assortment of drums and other music equipment that could topple at any minute. I'm a drummer in the orchestra, or show band as it is often called, and so I'm one of the musicians you see if you watch any of the production shows in the main theater. If you're on a cruise right now, we're the ones dressed in all black like we're going to a funeral, the ones walking around like we don't have anything to do. If you don't see any of us, go and check in the crew bar. We are probably in there drinking.

The show band is also the backup band for the various entertainers that perform aboard the cruise ship. This includes singers, magicians, jugglers, contortionists, banjo players, and accordion virtuosos (yes, there is such a thing, and it can be painful to watch). The show band also performs jazz sets in the cigar bar and a variety of other styles of music in the different venues around the ship. The orchestra is kind of the work horse of musicians on the ship— the one-stop shop for all your musical needs.

I was trying to move my drum set to the atrium for one of our biweekly jazz sets. We actually played more of an odd mix of funky tunes and Dixieland classics, but we'll call it jazz for the sake of simplicity. For these jazz set gigs, I had to move my entire drum set from one side of the ship to another twice a week.

Have you ever tried to walk from one end of a cruise ship to the other as fast as you can? If you're on a cruise right now, go do it and come back to me. Ok, that wasn't much fun was it? Remember all those people walking around aimlessly that were in your way? You know how I know all those people were there? Because they are always there. The *cones* are always there. On cruise ships, there is an entirely esoteric lingo that crew members use, and *cones* are what we call passengers. I'm not sure where the meaning derived, but I assume it is because crew members always feel like passengers are in the way, just aimlessly walking, gawking, and searching for the midnight buffet or something.

Back on the promenade, I'm pushing the cart of drums, and not a single *cone* is getting out of the way. The entire drum set had been unable to fit on the cart, so I'm also carrying a case of cymbals in one hand while trying to direct the cart through a crowd of passengers with the other hand. It was a comical course of immovable human obstacles. I make it about halfway across the ship after nearly clipping a few brightly-colored frozen drinks from a couple wearing matching tropical shirts. The couple looks like they could have come directly from a *Magnum PI* episode—one of the early ones before there was a decent budget. I continue to slowly steer my cart through the crowd, and then I see her from across the promenade. She has that look, that annoying inquisitive twinkle in her eyes. I cringe. I've been spotted and identified as an employee. I just know it. Before I can avoid her by quickly steering the teetering luggage cart behind one of the doors that lead into a "Crew Only" area, she's already across the promenade and tapping me on the shoulder.

"Do you work here?" she asks. I look at my name badge and then at the ridiculously heavy cart of drums.

"Yes Ma'am, what can I help you with?"

"Are you a musician?" I thought the name badge that clearly said "Musician" and the cart of drums would have given it away.

"Well, I guess I am," I said. The lame attempt at humor was met without reaction.

"Do you know where my room is?"

"Well, what is your room number?"

"I don't know."

Sigh... "I really wish I could help you. I have a performance in about thirty minutes, but I recommend you go to the Purser's desk. It is forward of the atrium, on the starboard side."

"Where is that?"

"Forward. Starboard. Mid ship."

"Which way is the front of the ship? Is that what you mean by forward? Star what? Where's the middle of the ship?"

This went on for five more minutes and then continued for five more years. It happened almost every time I would peek out of the crew area and find myself face-to-face with passengers. It can be exhausting, but this is part of the job. And believe me, there are many reasons to absolutely love this job. The midnight buffet is just one of them. I don't care how much people make fun of the midnight buffet. The midnight buffet is at midnight, 12 a.m. sharp, it rocks, and it is one of the great parts of working on a cruise ship. In fact, the musicians in the orchestra usually get off work around midnight, and the midnight buffet is often the first stop. Actually, there was a predictable order of events every day during the five years I worked on a cruise ship as a musician. I would sleep, eat, go to the gym, get off the ship and explore if we were in port, play music, hit the midnight buffet, party in the crew bar. Repeat for five years. However, the fascinating story of what it is like to work on a cruise ship is what happens between the obvious, and that is what we are going to explore in this book.

"What time is the midnight buffet?" was a question that never bothered me. In fact, I'm not certain I was ever asked that one. But I did reach the breaking point from the constant questions after two weeks. As a result, I, and a few other musicians on the cruise ship, joked about doing something about it. We thought it would be a great idea for the cruise company to print up some shirts for the crew to wear. We wanted the shirts to be printed with all of the stupid questions the crew gets asked, and then have extremely sarcastic answers printed below them. When we would get asked a stupid question, we could just point to the shirt and move on with our day. At one point, the company started threatening to do something entirely similar, but with the exact opposite outcome we had wanted. Some no-brain executive thought it would be a great idea to make shirts for the crew that had a giant question mark printed on them and in big letters, "How Can I Help You?" printed on the back. The company printed some of these shirts and handed them out to a few willing crew members to test the waters. They insisted that at least one crewmember from every department would have to take on the new roll of the walking and talking customer service agent. No one in the band would volunteer. Musicians don't volunteer for anything on the ship. We have enough work keeping sharp on our instruments as it is.

Eventually, they forced one of the guys in the band to take the shirt. I think he was our bass player. He didn't go into guest areas for the next month until the program was scrapped. The shirt was then promptly thrown overboard in an elaborate, highly illegal, and exceptionally intoxicated ceremony somewhere off the coast of Jamaica. I always hope to visit Jamaica someday and see some kid wearing the shirt after finding it washed up on the shore of Montego Bay. Do you have any idea how many times that kid would be asked if he knows where to get some pot?

"What time is the midnight buffet?" is really a silly question though, because the cruise ship is one giant, floating midnight buffet. The midnight buffet is whenever you want it to be. The midnight buffet is really no different than the buffet that happens the rest of the day. Sure, there are a few lull hours when the buffet is closed in an attempt to encourage the passengers to get out and do something other than eat. But if you want to eat during the lull when the buffet is closed, there are plenty of other choices. You have the dining rooms that serve you three meals a day. Then there are the buffets that also happen three times a day in case you miss your dining room opportunities or just feel like eating six times a day while you're on vacation. If you still want to eat more, you can visit the grill on the lido deck and stuff yourself full of hamburgers, hot dogs, fries, and gyros. You have the sandwich shops and the 24-hour pizzeria. On most ships there are sushi stands, steak houses, Italian restaurants, and a window café that serves a rotating list of Asian menus.

It's insane how much food there is on a cruise ship. It really is an incredible feat. On average, 105,000 meals are prepared every single week aboard a cruise ship. This requires around 20,000 pounds of beef, 12,000 pounds of chicken, and 28,000 eggs. So before you go out on your next cruise ship and find the show band drummer just to ask him, "What time is the midnight buffet?," I'm going to save the drummer from having to answer one more question. The midnight buffet is whenever you want it to be. And it never ends.

2

HOW DO YOU GET A JOB ON A CRUISE SHIP?

I always envisioned myself in my imaginary life at sea as a pirate on a plank-walking and danger-fraught adventure to Tahiti in search of trunks of gold, and I always had the hot blonde from *WKRP in Cincinnati* as my sidekick. That's just the way I envisioned it. I think most of us dream of a life at sea during some point in our lives. When we do, the life we imagine is often a highly romanticized version. But in truth, those pirates didn't have it so good. Even before we were sending care packages stuffed with missiles to the pirates in Somalia, a pirate's life wasn't all rum, swashbuckling, dark eye-shadow, and wrestling-giant-squid fun. Pirates had to suffer through squalls in high seas, hardtack Thanksgiving dinners, and months without women. It's not so different today really, unless the call to go to sea is a call to a luxury cruise liner. Well, the hardtack Thanksgiving dinner is about right.

For me, the call to the sea came out of the blue. The call came in on my cell phone, and it caught me completely off guard. I never tried to get a job on a cruise ship. I had never even been on a cruise before I spent five years on one. The job was just offered to me. I had spent my whole life in Pensacola on the coast of Florida, and I could count on two fingers the amount of times I had stepped foot onto a sailboat. Even after working as a musician for fifteen years, I had never met anyone else who had worked on a cruise ship.

Most people who become cruise ship crew members don't simply have the job just fall in their lap. Getting a job on a cruise ship usually starts when you walk into a recruiting office. There are recruiting offices all over the world from Mumbai to Mexico City. Recruitment agents pass out glossy pamphlets that paint ship life as the proverbial land of opportunity—a life filled with windfall paydays, all- you-can-eat cheesecake buffets, and endless days spent on sunny islands, lathered in cocoa butter, where the only work you do is on your tan. The Internet itself is packed with these types of agents. There are agents for housekeepers, cooks, social hosts, dancers, and even musicians. For every job on the cruise ship, there is an agent online who is more than happy to completely misrepresent what ship life is like and get you to sign a contract that puts 20 percent or more of your wages into their pockets.

Don't do it. If you want to work on a ship, get online and contact the cruise lines directly. Almost every cruise ship company has e-mail addresses and phone numbers right there on their websites for people who are looking to work out at sea. In most situations, you don't need an agent to get a job on a cruise ship. Granted, there are some cruise companies that prefer to hire through agents, so sometimes an agent will be your best bet. If you're interested in working in the entertainment department as a musician, dancer, or singer, you can contact most cruise lines directly and set up an audition, or find out when and where the next auditions will be held. If you don't pass the audition, this would be the recommended time to contact an agent and see if they might be able to help you out.

I'm going to say it right here. Before I get into all of the absolutely obnoxious aspects of what it is like to work on a cruise ship, I am going to say that if you want to work on a cruise ship—do it. It is a blast. There is nothing like it in the world, and if you find yourself dreaming of working out at sea on one of those massive party ships, then follow your dreams and go do it. You might have to suffer through food that looks like chicken beak stew. You might have to physically restrain yourself from killing passengers at the endless boat drills. You may have to perfect your duct tape skills in order to repair the machines in the crew laundry that are so rusty, they look as if they were pulled from the wreckage of the *Titanic*. Yet, you *will* have those days on perfect islands where the only work you have to do is on your tan. If you try, you will have a blast.

For me, the call to the sea came out of the blue. I never even thought that working on a cruise ship was a job that I could do as a musician. I figured, *if you want to work as a musician on a cruise ship you have to know how to read music really, really well. You have to be able to play all different styles of music, own a clean suit, a snazzy bow tie, and have a respectable collection of tropical shirts.* You do have to know how to read music really, really well, and I didn't. You do have to know how to play all the musical styles. I'm talking Motown, rock and roll, jazz, Latin, funk, reggae, calypso, Broadway, gospel, and most importantly a two-beat polka feel, and I didn't. You do have to own a partially clean suit and a snazzy clip-on bow tie, and I didn't. For the most part, the ship provides the tropical shirts. I only owned the token one I picked up in Hawaii.

I was working as a staff writer in Northwest Florida at the *Pensacola News Journal.* I was actually working in one of the satellite offices north of town. I guess it's where they send the rookies until they lose their greenhorn status. I had a great boss and fun coworkers. I loved the job. It was something different every day, a new story every minute. I had my own desk for the first time. Someone was actually paying me to sit and write. Right around the corner, Mama Bass's Kwik Burger was serving up the best southern cookin' in the south. There was free coffee at the office and fresh pecan pie down at Mama Bass's, so I was in heaven.

It was my last day at the newspaper job. In the middle of the newsroom, a scanner quietly broadcasted all of the local law enforcement transmissions to a mostly uninterested collection of journalists. We were all busy creating a chorus of keyboard typing and muffled phone interviews when the announcement came over the scanner.

The scanner beeped and then we heard a muffled voice announce, "Calling all available personnel, fire in progress at…"

My boss poked his head out of his office door.

"Josh, you get this one. It's your turn." He didn't say this in a way that was like, *Go get 'em tiger; you've earned your wings.* It was more like, *Travis got the last one, and he doesn't want to go, so, we're sending you.*

I was totally ecstatic. I was getting sent out to cover a real fire with fire trucks, fire chiefs, Dalmatians, potential arson conspiracies, and smoking guns. This was like real journalist shit. *Wow! Maybe I'll find the remnants of a Molotov cocktail in the ashes. I'd better bring the good camera.*

When I arrived, I found the remains of a fire that had started in the garage and quickly swept through the entire house. There was nothing left at this point but the charred frame of the house. There wasn't a single flame. What was left of the house was still smoking, but only a little. Strewn across the front lawn was a lumpy fire hose that was slowly leaking out of the end. A couple was sitting under a tree in the side yard looking absolutely stunned. The fire chief was still there too. He saw me coming from a mile away with my voice recorder, wrinkled shirt, Walmart tie, and tortoise-shell glasses. I had to go and stick my little hand-held recorder in the face of people who had just lost everything and were still polishing off a box of Kleenex. I'm sure I was all bouncy and smiling as I usually was at that time, which probably just made matters worse.

It was my last day at the job, and I wanted a big story to go out on. I interviewed the fire chief, kicked around in the ashes for Molotov cocktails, and then headed back to the office with my "big" story about a garage fire and a few pictures of a lumpy hose.

Back at the office, I was wrapping it up slowly. I didn't want to rush into that next big thing just yet. I wanted to take a little time at the end of this chapter of life and savor it. So, I slowly wandered around the office drinking my last cup of free coffee, taking an extra long time to download my photos, and putting the finishing touches on my lumpy hose, garage fire story. Then, my cell phone rang.

"Hello, This is Josh," I said.

"Hey, Josh, my man, this is Gary. How you doin'?"

I hadn't heard from Gary in awhile. I had toured Europe with his band back in February 2004. The band performed for American troops stationed in the Mediterranean. We spent most of our time traveling across Italy, but we also made stops in Portugal, Egypt, Spain, Greece, Turkey, and France. We were hired through Armed Forces Entertainment, which (in a pointedly degrading way) is called the "non-celebrity" branch of the USO. It's hard enough being a musician with big dreams of playing sold out stadium tours, then end up with low paying gigs in local bars performing for the worst audience members since John Wilkes Booth. You don't really need someone pointing out that you're a "non-celebrity." Trust me. We know.

When I heard Gary's voice, a flood of memories from the Europe tour with Gary and the band flooded my mind. I smiled as I remembered the time the band missed our flight out of Cairo. We had to wait at the airport for seven hours until the next flight departed. While we waited, the same Kenny G. song was played on a loop the entire time. For seven hours. The same Kenny G. song. For seven god-awful hours.

I remembered the time that a group of Egyptian police armed with AK47's surrounded our tour bus, then boarded and demanded we pay them a bribe before they would let us go. Fortunately for us, a black army officer—who I firmly believe was actually Cuba Gooding, Jr. preparing for his next role in a military action movie—jumped up and told the AK47-toting Egyptians that it was in their best interests not to mess with the fucking US Army. The police quickly left the bus and we drove off down the dusty roads of Egypt to our next gig somewhere in the Gaza Strip.

"Gary, I'm doing great. How are you? I'm just finishing up with work for the day. What's going on man?"

"I'm doing pretty good," Gary said (yes, I know Gary occasionally converses with improper grammar. No letters please). Everything Gary said was kind of under his breath and relaxed, which always made it seem like something was wrong. So when I thought something was wrong, at first I didn't think anything of it. He continued, "Listen, me and the band, we're out here working on a cruise ship in the Bahamas and we're having a little problem with our drummer. We want to know if you want to come out and join us."

"What? Wow! Thanks for thinking of me. Well, what kind of a gig is it?" I asked.

"Well, we play for like four hours a night with two nights off a week usually. We're doin' the same stuff we did on the tour, with maybe a few extra tunes. We rehearse about twice a week and try to add some new stuff—you know, to spice it up a little. It's an easy gig, but you have to play by the rules, and there are a lot of rules out here. The main thing is that we need a guy we can trust not to screw up—you know, break all the rules. I know we can trust you. You're a pretty clean-cut guy, and you're a good drummer that can do the job. You get fed and the food's all right, but you'll get sick of it eventually. You get a room. You'll probably be bunked with the show band drummer. That's where our last drummer was."

As usual, everyone always talks about the good stuff first. This was a mixed bag. He really sounded kind of down about the whole thing. He sounded really tired of it—tired of the food, tired of the gig or something. *How could anyone get tired of playing music on a cruise ship in the Bahamas? How could anyone get tired of free food?* I took a sip of my free coffee. I wasn't tired of that. Also, as usual, he had not mentioned money. It always comes last, although it's always the first thing on everyone's mind. The gig probably didn't pay beans. *I'll be lucky to get 1,200 bucks a month for this sort of gig,* I thought. Playing drums on a cruise ship in the Bahamas sounded like something most people would pay to do.

"That sounds great. What is the pay? And when do you want me out there?" I couldn't believe it. This was real musician shit. I hadn't heard from this guy in a year. I was packing up my office on the last day of my job at the newspaper, and out of the blue Gary calls me and asks if I want to go play drums on a cruise ship in the Bahamas.

"We need you out here as soon as possible. We're playing with a fucking drum machine right now, Josh. You would need to get a physical done, but I've talked to Brian. He's the guy you have to go through to get onboard, and he said we can fast track you if you want the job. We could get you out here in two weeks, hopefully sooner. The gig pays $2,600 a month, and the only thing you have to pay for is your alcohol and the stuff you want when we're in port. You can save a lot of money working out here if you try."

"This is great. It sounds like a blast. I love playing music with you guys, but how much time can you give me to think about it?"

"I can give you 'til later tonight. I've got to find someone fast, and there are a few other guys that I'm going to call after this that will probably take it. I know we can trust you not to screw up and break the rules though. The gig is yours if you want it. I can't promise it will be here later, but I can give you 'til later tonight.

I'll call you back later and see what you think."

The whole time Gary was talking, I imagined myself in a tropical shirt sipping a piña colada from the deck of a cruise ship. I was standing near the bow of the ship with the wind rushing all around me. I was surrounded by beautiful women in bikinis. Passengers were high-fiving me and saying, *"Hey, that's the drummer in the lounge band. You guys are awesome."* And then I thought about the endless free cups of coffee, the endless free slices of pecan pie, and the free whatever-the-hell-I-want to eat. I thought about what it would be like to only have to worry about playing drums and having fun.

"Gary, I don't need to think about it." I interrupted him mid-sentence and then impulsively made a decision that would change my life forever. It was a decision that would send me out to a life at sea for the next five years.

"I want the job."

3

WHAT IS IT LIKE TO WORK ON A CRUISE SHIP?

It's awesome, especially at first. That's the short, quick, and easy answer. But let's start from the beginning. When you sign up to work on a cruise ship, your work as a crew member doesn't start the day you step foot on the ship. Your work actually begins way before all of that. And it doesn't matter whether you are asked out of the blue to go and work on a cruise ship like I was, or you apply for the job through more traditional routes, there is quite an unexpected, head jarring, and exhausting process you must go through first. You have to complete an application and then the dreaded medical evaluation. The application is about as long as a James Michener novel, and the medical evaluation form is so exhaustive and detailed, I would be willing to bet that the form is identical to the one NASA gives to astronauts to ensure they are fit to go into space. And not only is the medical evaluation insanely long, it is also outrageously expensive. However, the insanity of this process is merely an apt introduction to the madness and bureaucracy that you will encounter on a daily basis while living aboard a cruise ship.

I got in touch with Brian. He was in charge of helping me complete the paper work I needed to finish before I could actually step foot on the ship. He desperately was trying to fast track me so I could relieve the band from their drum machine nightmare that had them sounding like a bad version of the Talking Heads. If you don't know who the Talking Heads are, then put down this book, download one of their tunes (something other than "Once in a Lifetime" please), and then keep reading. You'll thank me for it later. I promise.

Brian emailed me the Charles Dickens novel disguised as a medical evaluation form. I took it up to the local clinic. The doctor's jaw dropped when he saw the stack of paper I had carried in with me. The medical evaluation required a chest x-ray and complete blood work for nearly every communicable disease known to man. The doctor couldn't believe how extensive it was. I couldn't believe the cost. The exam was going to cost me $1,100! I reluctantly forked over the cash.

At the time, I didn't understand why the cruise ship company would go to such great lengths to ensure that crew members are healthy before stepping onto a ship. But now I understand after spending five years working on cruise ships. I've been aboard when crew members have died or become seriously ill. This can cost the cruise ship companies big bucks. As an example, a trombone player in the orchestra developed appendicitis while we were out floating in the middle of the ocean. Earlier in the day, the trombone player and I had gone hiking somewhere around the Bay of Fundy in Canada. That afternoon, we had been eating cheeseburgers and laughing. A few hours later, he's in the ship's clinic looking like he's at death's door. They had to land a helicopter onto the deck of the cruise ship and Life Flight him to a hospital in Boston for surgery before his appendix burst. One morning, my neighbor in the cabin next to me woke up to find his roommate, a Ukrainian piano player, dead in his bed. The Ukrainian musician had died of a heart attack while he was sleeping. There are stories of crew members falling over board and getting sucked into the propellers of the ship, people falling down flights of stairs, show band musicians dying of alcohol poisoning in their sleep after taking exceptional advantage of the cheap booze in the crew bar. When crew members die on board, it's devastating. For the cruise company, it's also expensive because when crew members die on board, their families call the lawyers. So, maybe it's in the best interests of the cruise ship companies to do their homework and make sure they recruit exceptionally healthy employees who carry the lowest possible financial liability and risk. Unfortunately, the result is that crew members are required to perform these extensive and often extremely expensive medical evaluations.

After the medical evaluation was completed, I was extremely glad to get that part of the job over with. Yet, I have to admit, it was hard for me to understand why the cruise company couldn't just perform the medical evaluation aboard one of their cruise ships, especially since almost every cruise ship on the seven seas is equipped with a fully staffed clinic. Giving me the opportunity to get my medical evaluation performed aboard one of their ships by one of their hundreds of doctors sure would have been a nice gesture before I went out and busted my ass for them for the next six months. Then again, I guess there are a lot of things I don't understand about cruise ships. I was just happy that I would never have to do that medical evaluation again. Unfortunately, the feeling was fleeting. A few months into my first contract, a fellow crew member informed me that I was required to complete a medical evaluation every two years. Ouch!!! Worse still, I discovered that if I took a break from working on a ship that lasted longer than three months, I would have to pay $1,100 again and complete another medical that was the length of a Webster's dictionary. Even so, I wasn't about to let a $1,100 membership fee ruin my good time on club cruise ship, and it didn't.

I was assigned to a cruise ship sailing out of Fort Lauderdale, which is about 30 miles north of Miami. Fort Lauderdale is very much like Miami, except it has absolutely none of the good qualities that you would find in Miami and hardly any positive attributes that you would desire in a coastal Florida city. When you are a crew member in Fort Lauderdale, the highlight of your day ashore occurs when you are corralled into a van with twenty other rather smelly crew members for an excursion to the local Walmart. Of course, I was blissfully unaware of my fate. Fort Lauderdale sounded exotic and tropical. So, I was really excited about being assigned to that particular home port.

I was living eight hours away from Fort Lauderdale in Pensacola. And since I would be playing with the lounge band on the ship, I needed to bring my own drum set. The drummers who perform with the orchestra and jazz bands on the ships are the lucky ones. They are provided with a drum set. This is a drummer's dream come true. In those situations, drummers only need to bring a pair of drumsticks aboard the cruise ship. However, I had to provide all of my own equipment. This meant that I needed to drive my car down to the Fort Lauderdale port. Given what happened later, I would be extremely happy I did this.

I packed my drums into the car, but then I was stumped. I stopped cold. I had no idea what to bring on a cruise. I grabbed a suitcase and threw in a few pairs of swim shorts, a tux I had recently purchased from Goodwill, a snazzy clip-on bow tie, and a few bottles of sunscreen. But then I just didn't know what else to pack. I had never been on a cruise. I had no idea what to expect and no idea how to prepare for my job on the cruise ship. What do you pack for a six-month cruise?

I was assigned to a ship that was sailing in the

Bahamas. The ship's itinerary was going to alternate between three- and four-day cruises. We would start out in Fort Lauderdale, leaving around five o'clock in the afternoon, and then cruise all night 'til we reached Nassau in the Bahamas. We would spend seven hours in port in Nassau, which is plenty enough time to get thoroughly tired of the place, unless a plastic-looking casino modeled after the fabled sunken city of Atlantis is your idea of a good time. We would then head back out to sea and bob around in the Caribbean until we landed at Half Moon Cay, a private island owned by Carnival Corporation, the next morning. If it was a three-day cruise, we would spend the rest of the cruise navigating back to Fort Lauderdale. On a four day-cruise, we would spend the extra day on the island of Grand Turk in the Turks and Caicos. The schedule sounded like heaven to me. But I had no idea what to pack. Would I need a six-month supply of Dramamine? Would there be a music store where I could buy new drumsticks in the Caribbean? What if I didn't like the food? Would I need to pack a supply of noodle cups and Snickers bars that could last for six months just in case?

I packed an extra bottle of sunscreen. This brought the total to five big bottles. I threw in about ten pairs of mostly chewed up drumsticks and an extra set of earplugs. I didn't know how much I would be working on the ship either. I thought it was most likely that I would be working most of the time. However, I thought there was the possibility that I might have a substantial amount of free time with nothing to do on the ship. I figured I could bring a few books along. *Yeah, books are a great idea. I'll have tons of time with nothing to do on the ship. Books will be perfect.*

I packed a lot of books; I mean *a lot* of books. I packed two medium-sized duffel bags full of books. I love to read, and I figured this was my chance. This was going to be the adventure of a lifetime, and I wanted to be prepared to waste it in the bindings of hand-me-down paperbacks.

After I finished packing, I lay down on my bed one last time and began to fantasize about my new life that was just about to begin out on the cruise ship. I imagined myself out at sea. I saw myself standing inside a very well-appointed cabin. Foamy waves were crashing against a large porthole window. To one side of the room, I imagined a large, plush bed outfitted with a comforter that had been hand stitched with images of light houses, ship bells, and a man with a beard wearing a yellow rain slicker. There was a dim yellow light coming from a pair of antique brass ship's lanterns that were bolted onto miniature, wooden ship wheels. There were wall-to-wall teak floors and metal rails that were polished to a perfect shine. My crew cabin looked more like the interior of a Red Lobster restaurant than any room I had ever seen, and it was so stunningly spacious that it gave a whole new meaning to the term open floor-plan. In one corner of the room was a cedar-framed hot tub large enough for four people to stretch out in. I imagined myself in the hot tub reading passages from *Moby Dick*. I would occasionally pause from my reading, fetch a collapsible brass spotting scope, and observe the whales cresting from the foamy sea outside my porthole window. This is what I imagined my crew cabin on the cruise ship would be like. Boy was I wrong.

When I finished packing my car, I had weighed it down with enough books to equal the body weight of the fat Drew Cary. I needed to be in Fort Lauderdale by 10 a.m. in order to have enough time to load my luggage and gear onto the ship; so I started driving towards my new ship life at two in the morning. I had no idea what to expect. All Gary had told me was that there were going to be a lot of rules, and that we were going to have a lot of fun. I'm able to follow rules just fine. Playing music with Gary was always fun. Besides, how could I not have a blast while getting paid $2,600 a month to play music on a giant party ship that was navigating to some of the most beautiful islands in the world? This was going to be all right.

Nonetheless, I started to get nervous the minute I pulled through the gates to the Fort Lauderdale port. This was a huge change. I hadn't really thought this through. I was committing to the next six months to live on this...and then there it was—a hump like a snow hill with a giant, funny shaped, red and blue smoke stack towering from the lido deck. It was my new home for the next six months, and it was massive. Nothing could have prepared me for how big it was going to be. I had no idea that these ships were so unbelievably large, and apparently this was one of the smaller ships in the fleet. It was called the *Fantasy*. I could not have hand picked a better name for my first ship. This *was* the Fantasy.

I found the bass player for the band waiting for me in the parking lot. Everyone just called the bass player Star Man—a name that at once aptly reflected his substantial star quality as a musician and his seemingly unmatched ego. Star Man helped perpetuate a rumor that he had once toured with Prince by telling this to everyone willing to talk with him. He also claimed to have grown up in the same neighborhood as Victor Wooten, who is the bassist for the virtuoso banjo player named Bela Fleck. His story was that he learned everything Victor Wooten knew about the bass. After hearing him play, there was absolutely no reason to doubt him. The guy could slap the bass guitar funkier than anyone I had ever heard. This guy was cookin'. I had worked with Star Man before in different bands around Pensacola. I couldn't wait to get on stage with him again and lock into the groove. I grabbed a few of my drums, and he offered to carry a few of my bags. He grabbed the two duffel bags full of books.

"Man, what you got in here, bro?"

"Books. I figured I should bring a couple in case I get bored." Star man chuckled under his breath in his *you're-a-complete-idiot* kind of way. He looked at me.

"Trust me Josh. You're not gettin' bored on my ship. This is *my* ship. I own this ship, and you're not getting' bored out here. If you get bored here, you might as well give up. Because if you can't have fun on a cruise ship, then you can't have fun *anywhere*."

He turned out to be right. I never opened up a book the whole time I was aboard the *Fantasy*. I was too busy having fun. So, I was wrong about the books. I was also wrong about the extent of luxurious amenities that I would find in my crew cabin. Dead wrong.

Even from a distance, the ship looked huge. When we stood beside it, the side of the ship rose to the sky like a towering, white, metal canyon wall. We muscled my drums, books, and bottles of suntan lotion up the steep, clanking, metal gangway. Once we reached the top of the gangway, we entered the ship through a large opening in the ship's side. In a way, it was a threshold from which I would never return. When I passed through this threshold, I began a transformation from landlubber to seaman, from a citizen of the United States to a cruise ship crew member, from my life of loosely structured schedules and taken-for-granted freedoms to a life of regimented itineraries and hierarchical governance. It was a magical threshold that led from real life to ship life.

I walked onto the ship and was met by a security guard. When you first board a cruise ship as a crew member, you are required to send all of your personal belongings through an x-ray machine. This was my first encounter with a cruise ship security guard, and it was about as pleasant as each of the 10 million experiences that I would have with ship security guards over the next five years. First off, for some reason nearly every security guard is Indian, not Native American, but India Indian. The reasons for this will be thoroughly addressed in Chapter 6 which is titled "Why Are All the Officers Italian?," but for now just believe it. It's true.

The security guard patted me down, and then he stuffed everything I had through a flimsy looking x-ray machine. There was no hello, no welcoming gesture, and no pat on the back for suffering through my medical and finally making it onto the cruise ship; there was just an exhausted looking Indian guy with bags under his eyes who grabbed my luggage and threw it onto the conveyor belt. Another security guard was standing beside the x-ray machine. He approached me and began to pat me down. I felt like I was entering a prison. What next, they're going to take me to the delousing unit? The security guard behind the machine was watching a small screen that revealed the contents of my luggage. He pushed a button and the conveyer belt stopped, and then he pushed another button and the conveyer belt reversed direction. I watched my bags slowly back out of the machine. My bags had been rejected. The security guard had a serious look on his face, although it was no different than the look he had when I had first got onboard the ship.

"Upin-jew-ba-blee," the security guard said and started pointing towards my luggage. *What the heck did he just say?* I thought. He began pointing frantically to my luggage.

"Upin-jew-ba-blee," he said again. This time his big, brown head was rocking back and forth on his shoulders like the top of a bobble head that just got flicked.

"I'm sorry, what?" I said. The security guard looked at me square in the eyes and then repeated himself— this time talking in slow, individual words as if I was a child with a severe learning disability.

"Upin. Jew. Bag. Blease."

"Ah, open my bag please. Yes, no problem. Sorry." I felt like an asshole. I was holding up the line of crew members behind me as well. When I turned around, I realized everyone else waiting in line felt like I was an asshole too. I opened one of my suitcases. The security guard rummaged around and then pulled out a half-empty bottle of rum I had packed at the last minute.

"You cannot bring this aboard," he said. I was shocked. What kind of a cruise ship won't let you take rum aboard? My entire perception of sailors had been forged by repetitive rides on Pirates of the Caribbean at Disney World. I wasn't sure if I wanted to go on the Mormon version of the ride.

"I can't bring a bottle of rum onto the cruise ship?" I asked.

"No, it has to be unopened. This bottle is opened. You no can bring this rum aboard," he said.

"OK, well, I guess I will make sure and bring full bottles onboard from now on."

"Dank you," he said and waved his hand for me to step aside. I felt better now. This was more like it. I made a note to myself to pick up a bottle of Havana Club as soon as we reached Grand Cayman.

My luggage was pushed through the x-ray machine. I walked past the security station and stepped into a crew area for the first time. I have to admit that my expectations of what I would find in the crew area may have been unreasonably high. I was expecting the *Titanic*. Not a devastating iceberg collision scenario, but grand and pretentious ballrooms with rows of crystal chandeliers, every gentleman aboard parading the promenade in a finely fitted tuxedo, people calling me sir in a snooty British accent as they offered me palm-tree-shaped slices of *pâté* from silver platters, and red carpeted spiraling staircases with an endless march of slender and sexy bachelorettes dressed in gorgeous sparkling evening gowns sliding down the rails.

However, what I saw when I stepped into the crew area for the first time was a place that closely resembled a really cheap two-star motel with old carpet and extremely poor lighting. There were people everywhere and the crew members walking around represented nearly every nationality. All of them were briskly walking in one direction or the other down a long cavernous hallway that stretched the entire length of the ship. There were forklifts hauling soaring piles of luggage. The forklifts were parting the crowd as they zoomed back and forth, barely squeezing through the hallway. They were loaded down with enormous boxes of tenderloin, bags of flour, and more bananas than I had ever set my eyes on at one given time. The hallway I was standing in is called the I-95 by crew members, and this is the main artery and causeway for traffic among the hundreds of branching hallways within the labyrinth of the ship's crew area.

The sound of the crew members talking was overwhelming. I could hear what sounded like almost every language of the world in this hallway. Most prominently were the sounds of Indian, Filipino, Italian, Russian, and English. Just a few seconds ago I was in America. I was standing in Fort Lauderdale, Florida. Now I was standing somewhere that looked and sounded like a completely different world. When I crossed through the threshold of that ship at the top of that clanking gangway, I had stepped into an entirely different city where everyone wore a uniform and a name tag, no one had even a trace of stubble on their faces, and there was a lot of short, spiky, over-gelled hair. There were a lot of smiles, but I saw a lot of exhaustion underneath those smiles. It was like stepping onto a really busy sidewalk in New York City that is encased inside of a Walmart distribution warehouse with really bad overhead fluorescent lighting. It was a place where everyone shaved and wore the same clothes every day. It was a place where everyone got their hair cut by the same barber, and the only hair product available in the world was gel. I had stepped into a whole new society that had an entirely new and unique culture, and it smelled really, really bad.

The smell of the crew area is a very special thing. It is like nothing else on the planet, and I mean that. The scent is complex, like a bouquet of bad smelling flowers. In the foreground is the unmistakable stench of body odor. Believe it or not, there are some cultures on the planet that find body odor to be inoffensive. Let's just say some of these cultures make up a large segment of the employees on cruise ships. I swear that there is a recruiting agent somewhere that has an extremely foul sense of humor. He recruits only the worst smelling people that walk into his well-ventilated office, and then he sends them all directly to the ship that I am currently working on. At times, the ship can be like a train ride in Paris on a hot summer day—only worse. Underneath all of the body odor is the smell of wet paint. From what I have observed, I have drawn the conclusion that painting is at the very core of religious activity for a cult of crew members that wear white overalls. Fresh paint is constantly being applied somewhere on the ship. Sometimes, it appears as if the cruise ship officers are simply giving crew members senseless work because there is nothing else for them to work on at the time. I've observed tired men in splattered overalls painting over perfectly bright-white railings that I know had just been painted the day before. As a result, the ship is almost always circulating the smell of fresh, wet, white paint.

Blending with the smells of fresh paint and body odor is the fantastic scent of cigarette smoke. When I first started working on ships, the crew could only smoke in their cabins and at designated smoking areas that were usually located in open-air breezeways. However, the smoking rules were very loosely enforced, and back then it was very common to see a crew member casually walking down the hallway in a crew area just flicking ashes on the ground and puffing a cigarette, or see a group of Eastern Bloc casino employees huddled around a doorway having a contest to see who could chain-smoke the most cigarettes in an hour before their break was up. It was awful, and thank God they have changed the rules (at least some companies have).

Rounding out the complex fragrances of our "Crew Area" cologne was a strong note of rancid food. The smell seemed to be coming from down the hall to my left side. I would later discover that this was, unfortunately, where the crew mess was located. However, the smell seemed to be coming from the nearby garbage room where several very unfortunate crew members spend more than ten hours a day doing nothing but sorting through every bit of discarded food and garbage that is generated by the cruise ship. Then again, maybe the smell was coming from the crew mess. I'm still not sure about that.

Star Man and I shuffled our way through the crowd and across the I-95, nearly getting flattened by a forklift carrying enough corn to run a Frito Lay plant for a week. The forklift was carrying bushels upon bushels. I was amazed. This was just the beginning of what I would see on the cruise ship that day that absolutely amazed me, and most of it did so in an entirely pleasant way. On the other side of the hall was a large stairwell. We began our descent into the depths of the ship. When I boarded the ship, I was just about at waterline. Now, I was headed below the waterline; beneath the surface of the sea where the crew lives, and where I would be living for the next six months.

We descended below the waterline, passing deck after deck. Each level looked nearly identical, a seemingly endless maze of tan walls, tan doors, and a series of stairwells that broke up the monotony every 100 feet or so. Each stairwell looked as if it had been painted white about fifteen minutes or so before we got onboard. We lugged my bags down three levels. As we descended into the lower decks of the ship, I could feel the air getting stuffier, and I could see and smell the air becoming smokier too.

The hallways were tiny—barely enough room for two people to pass each other without rubbing shoulders. Coming from deep within the bowels of the ship were the ratcheting, grinding, rumbling sounds of machinery that made the walls vibrate and the ceiling hum. The ceiling above us had no insulation or soundproofing whatsoever. The sounds of the footsteps from crew members walking on the deck above us were so loud you would believe they were wearing wooden-soled shoes. I hoped with all my heart that we would turn a corner and find the captain there waiting to greet me into an area of the ship that was much cleaner, much newer, much more spacious, and much less smelly. I imagined a large wooden door with a shiny brass plaque on the front that read, "Lounge Band Drummer." Behind the door I would find the hot tub, the teak floors, and my trusty spotting scope waiting for me.

Instead, we arrived at a tan door just like every other tan door in the hallway. There are these seminal moments in one's life when we wake up and realize that we are in fact no more special than anyone else. For me, this was one of those moments. We walked up to a door that was surrounded with bright-red trim. The door was covered in filthy fingerprints. My name was printed on a small paper card that was tucked into a plastic sleeve beside the door. There was no brass plaque. The captain was nowhere in sight. Star Man handed me the key to my room which looked like a plastic credit card. I placed the key in a slot on the door handle, heard the door unlock, and opened the door.

I was wrong about the room. Dead wrong. There were no teak floors. Instead, there was tan colored wall-to-wall vinyl that was ripped and chipped in many places. Standing in the doorway I could nearly touch my bed, but I could definitely touch the bathroom. The bathroom was right next to the room's entrance. It was so small that from where I was standing in the doorway to the room, I could nearly reach across the entire length of the bathroom, touch the back wall, and still have a little arm length left. I couldn't believe it was possible to fit a toilet, sink, and shower in such a small space. These bathrooms were apparently designed by a draftsman who can write people's names on grains of rice, or someone who specializes in designing entire homes that can fit into sardine cans. On the far wall, (which is way too strong a word for the distance) was my bed which was the bottom half of a bunk bed that was about as wide as a countertop. I hadn't slept in a bunk bed since I was eight years old. There was definitely no hot tub. In fact, a hot tub would have taken up all the remaining free space in the room. The room was more than a let down; it was a huge disappointment. In fact, I thought it was ridiculous. And where was my porthole window? There was no porthole window. There was no square window. There was no rectangular window. There was no window at all. Just a tan wall with a tiny desk, a scratched up wardrobe, a single chair in the middle of the room, and my roommate's clothes spread out in a particularly annoying and random fashion. *At least it's free,* I thought. *That's the spirit, Josh! This isn't a windowless sardine can with a bunk bed for a room. It's a free windowless sardine can with a bunk bed for a room, and it's yours. This will be all right. Who needs a window anyway? I can go out on the breezeway and look across the sea and breathe that fresh sea air as much as I like. I'd probably get tired of staring out at that boring old sea after a few months anyway, and besides, I'm getting paid for this.*

With that, I accepted my fate. I would be living in this sardine can, and I would be happy. I threw down my bags and was ready for Star Man's grand tour of the gigantic ship, my new home. Star Man and I headed back up the stairwell above the waterline where the air was fresher.

We marched down the I-95 towards the middle of the ship. Star Man turned around and looked back at me as he dodged forklifts and Filipinos.

"You ever been on a cruise ship, Josh?" Star Man asked.

"Not until today."

"Let's check out the Lido deck, and then we got to get you set up, get a sound check done, and run through some tunes before we play tonight."

When I first got on board I had been handed a "Welcome Aboard" packet from the purser's office. They also issued me a name tag and informed me I had to wear this at all times, even while I was eating in the crew mess. It was like they were saying, "Welcome aboard. Now, we own your ass." As we walked, I flipped through the packet. There was a map of the ship that detailed both the crew and passenger areas. This ship was enormous. I thought it might take me a few days before I would learn my way around the ship. It ended up taking months. As I flipped through the welcome aboard packet, I came to a section that listed the dress code for crew members when we are in passenger areas. It was very specific and detailed in regards to what we were and were not allowed to wear: no closed-toe shoes, no jeans, only khakis or slacks, no tee shirts, only polo shirts or button-up dress shirts. On formal nights, men had to be in a suit and tie at all times; jacket on and tie snug. I looked over at Star Man as we climbed more steps towards a rather expensive looking wood-grain door. Across the front of the door were the words "Passenger Area." I looked at what Star Man was wearing. He had on flip-flops, swim trunks, and a sleeveless tee shirt. *So much for the rules. This place must be relaxed*, I thought. I was wrong. Wrong again. Star Man just didn't give a shit.

Star Man opened the door, and for a moment it was hard to believe these two vastly different worlds, the crew area and the passenger area, were connected only by a flimsy panel of wood. *This was more like it*, I thought. This was what I thought a cruise ship would be like and more. We were standing out on an expansive oval-shaped deck which was like a giant balcony that wrapped around the entire perimeter of the lido deck. For those of you who have never been on a cruise, the lido deck is the main outdoor deck on a cruise ship. It is where you will find the swimming pools, lounge chairs, hot tubs, water slides, and the wave pools where passengers can try a little artificial surfing after they have had too many strawberry daiquiris and right before they fall and break their back. And for all you people obsessed with trivia like I am, *lido* is actually an Italian word that means beach.

The Atlantic Ocean sparkled to one side of the ship. We were still docked, and on the other side of the ship I could see passengers slowly boarding. On the lido deck below us, and all around us on this upper level, people were exploring the ship for the first time. Most of the passengers were already holding frozen alcoholic drinks with little colorful umbrellas sticking out the top. Now, a word of advice to those of you on a cruise right now; any drink on a cruise that your bartender takes the time to decorate with any sort of umbrella, or cutesy chocolate ship's wheel, or plastic flamingo or something is going to be unbelievably expensive. And I speak the truth when I say that receiving a bar bill at the end of a cruise where you spent every day on the lido deck sucking down piña colada's before you asked how much they cost is the quickest way to have all of that relaxation that you experienced on your cruise sucked right of you. You should sneak Everclear aboard the cruise ship in water bottles like everyone else. That will bring the fun ship to a whole new level.

On the lido deck, there was a pair of pools and several hot tubs. There was a stage in the center of the deck where a reggae band was setting up for a performance during the sail away party. Behind us, there was a set of water slides. Kids were sailing down the tubes that sent them splashing into a pool of water. At one end of the deck, there were a few Filipino crew members cooking and serving up a steady stream of hot dogs, hamburgers, French fries, and gyros to passengers. I had never seen so many people with ice cream cones in their hands at one time in my life. People who looked as if they could fast for an entire week and still have plenty of fat reserves to run a marathon and then climb Mount Everest were already taking full advantage of the free food. Bikinis, swim suits, and sunglasses were the dress code here, and even though what I saw wasn't very pretty—I liked it.

"Can we swim in the pools?" I asked Star Man. This was a giant party, and I was ready to jump right in.

"No."

"Can we use the hot tubs?"

"No. But, we do have our own hot tubs for the crew. They're out on the crew deck in the front of the ship. Right in front of the crew bar."

"Well, that's not so bad," I said. Star Man looked as if he was scoping out all the women that had just boarded the cruise ship, but I couldn't be sure.

"This is it, man, your new home. Enjoy it while you can. We're gonna have a blast. Come on. I'll show you a little more of the ship."

We walked through a door that led to the interior of the ship. We were met with a blast of cold air. It felt like we were stepping into an ice box. You learn quickly as a crew member that the ship only has two temperatures. When the air conditioner is broken or off it's blazing hot. When the air conditioner is on, the interior of the ship in passenger areas is freezing cold. It's just the way it is on a cruise ship. There is no in between. Moderation is prohibited on a cruise ship, apparently. You can see this everywhere you look too. I realized that I would need to buy a jacket for when I was inside the ship. This is ridiculous, but crew members actually spend most of their time in the Caribbean wearing jackets. Star Man and I walked by expansive dining rooms with plaster sculptures, giant mural paintings of coral and tropical fish. Every rail looked like it was polished 100 times a day. They probably are. There were oversized porthole windows, like the one I imagined would be in my room, that lined the hallway and framed the ocean outside like a masterpiece oil painting. I smelled the air. It was crisp, cold, and pleasant smelling air. I could hardly believe the crew area was so nearby. Everything so far was so extremely elegant and so impressively designed.

However, the ship was built in the 1980s, so it was a little dated. There was a little too much neon, and some of the clubs and other rooms looked as if a Debbie Gibson outfit had exploded and permanently attached itself to the walls and furniture. Yet, at the same time, it was jaw dropping to think that all of this was part of one ship. The bars along the promenade had bar tops made of granite, leather swiveling stools, and massive wine racks mounted onto walls of glass that were back-lit with purple lights. In the atrium, I found that spiral staircase I had imagined as well as a colorful glass chandelier, which was clearly a Dale Chihuly rip-off (with spiraling whisker-things and all), hanging above a grand piano. It was all quite the classy affair—that is, until we got to the club where we would be performing.

The club was called The Cat's Meow. And whether at a glance, or after sitting in the room for hours contemplating what the hell was going on with this place, it made no sense whatsoever. Whoever designed it either must have literally been the worst interior designer ever, or worked for a PR firm representing both the cat food brand Meow Mix and Goodyear Tires. The club was atrocious. It was appalling. It was more fit for a bulldozer than any place I had ever set foot in. Yet, it was ours. This club was the place where we were supposed to make musical magic happen.

Surrounding the stage was a collection of the most ridiculous decorative decisions ever assembled in one room. Filling the club were round booths and tables. Printed on the outside of the round booths were canned cat food labels. So, when you walked into the club and sat down at a table, it looked like you were sitting inside a can of cat food. Why this would be appealing, I have no idea. All ten paintings on the wall were of giant bags of Meow Mix brand cat food. In the center of the bar was an elevated, circular dance floor that was designed to resemble a tire laid on its side flat on the ground. The Goodyear brand name was painted onto the tire/dance floor's surface. Here and there were neon geometric shapes; remnants of Debbie Gibson's outfit left over from other rooms that were thrown in for good measure, maybe to make the room appear even more confusing and disjointed than it already was. So, we had a dance floor shaped like a tire, cans of cat food for booths, and giant bags of cat food painted on the walls. The Cat's Meow made you feel like you were in a place, not where a cute kitty cat would come strolling into the club in a tight miniskirt, but inside of a re-creation of the scene where Debbie Gibson's cat got ran over. It was ridiculously strange, but we would make it work.

I needed to get a few things situated in my room, so we headed back down below the waterline into the dismal abyss and the stuffy air of the crew area. I was down there no longer than two minutes before I desperately missed the passenger area of the ship. As we walked towards my room, Star Man stopped. He looked up in the air as if he had just remembered something very important.

"Man, I gotta go get some milk," he said.

"What do you mean you have to go get some milk? Do I need to go get milk?" I asked. Star Man looked at me with a straight face.

"They've got the best milk on these ships. It's so good. But they always run out, and they always put a new bag in the machine at the beginning of the cruise. So, I gotta go fill up my milk jug before they run out. And don't come around here askin' for milk, cuz I ain't gonna give you none."

I didn't quite understand what he was saying, but I figured I should check out some of this milk. I also gathered that the food must be pretty bad if Star Man was having such concerns about whether he was going to get his milk or not. On ships, I would later learn, it was the little things that helped you get by, and you could get the little things by keeping track of the complex schedule on the ship. It is knowing things like what days of the week you can get into the gym or into the Laundromat without it being crowded, or when it will fit into your schedule to visit the Thai restaurant and get a bowl of *tom kha ghai*, or when you can get milk before it runs out. It is the little things that help you get by on a ship. And the little things are a big deal when you work on a cruise ship.

I stepped into my own private, sardine-can-of-a-bedroom and realized that there was a silver lining to the bathroom I had overlooked earlier. The good thing about the bathroom on cruise ships is that it is so small you can wash up, use the toilet, and lean over the sink to shave, all while standing in the shower. This was going to take some getting used to. Little did I know, I would have five years to get used to it. I never quite did, to be honest.

I was trying to get the rest of my books and clothes stuffed into the four drawers I had to my name when an announcement came over the loudspeaker that was mounted into the ceiling of my room.

"All crew member. All crew member." The voice was distinctly Italian and the English was very bad. Every few words would be interrupted with an "ah" which seems to be an Italian form of punctuation. "All crew-ah member, report to your-ah muster station-ah and prepare for the lifeboat drill-ah. At this time-ah, all crew member-ah, must report to their muster station for the boat drill-ah."

This was the beginning. This was the absolute beginning of my life being dictated by the whim of the cruise ship schedule, and the schedule was empowered to express itself at any waking moment through an obnoxious loudspeaker mounted into the ceiling of my sardine-can sized room. I had no idea at the time that these boat drills would continue, one or two a week depending on the length of the cruises, for the next five years. It is an understatement to say that these boat drills are no fun at all. In fact, they are so abhorrently miserable that I have spared you the description of what they are like here and will save that for the section on boat drills found in Chapter 8 that is titled "What is the Worst Part about Working on a Cruise Ship?"

After the boat drill was over, I was setting up my drum set in The Cat's Meow when I heard the ship's horn blow for the first time. I felt the ship leave the secure mooring of the Fort Lauderdale port. We were officially sailing, and minutes later I felt the sway of the ocean as the boat gently rocked back and forth on its bearing towards Nassau.

The band finished a sound check just in time for our first set. I was familiar with most of the material the band was performing, as most of it was what we had performed on our Europe tour. I fell right into place, and boy was it great to be on stage with that band again. We were packing the club the minute we started running through Earth, Wind, and Fire classics and belting out three-part harmonies on Aretha Franklin hits. The young female vocalist, Shelia, could sing anything, and she could work the crowd too. The guitar player, Gary, was a very rhythmic guitar player, and the band would lock into these great grooves that were held down tight by his funky and perfectly placed chord picking. Star Man was never in the shadows when he played. He slapped the bass so funky that it demanded attention. To this day, I don't think I've ever played with a bass player that took more solos on stage than Star Man, and the crowd loved every single one of them. His solos always received as much applause as when anyone else took a solo, and that's saying a lot for a bass solo. I apologize to all the bass players out there, but it's true. Just ask a guitar player, he'll tell you the same thing.

After that first gig was over, I was exhausted. As I walked back to my room, I could feel the ship swaying even more. I had to brace myself to keep from running into the walls in the hallway. I definitely hadn't found my sea legs yet. I settled into my bed and pulled the thin, solid-blue blanket over me. The sound of waves crashing onto the side of the ship surrounded the cabin. The room swayed in the gentle rocking of the ocean. Before I fell into a deep sleep, I felt ready, excited even, to wake up and do it all over again the next day.

And that is exactly what I did. I woke up, and then I did it all again the next day, and the next day, and the next day, for the next five years. If there is anything that can sum up what it is like to work on a cruise ship, it is that you live a life of repetition. I fell right into a groove of waking up in the morning, walking a few hundred feet to the crew mess, hanging out with the other musicians over breakfast, getting out and exploring the ports if it was a port day, going to the gym, getting warmed up and practicing on my instrument for a few hours, having lunch, playing the show, stopping by the crew bar for a few drinks, hanging out with the crew, and then heading back to bed.

Of course, this is just the schedule that I had. This is very different than the schedule that most cruise ship crew members have. I know that I have covered this next topic in the introduction, but I believe it is worth expanding on. It is intriguing to think about how everyone who has ever worked on a cruise ship has probably had a completely unique experience. And what type of experience a crew member has while working on a cruise ship has a lot to do with what type of job they have on the ship. A musician's experience is going to be very different from that of a ship photographer, or a cook, waiter, officer, dancer, doctor, or the captain.

However, it is my opinion that the crew members who work in the entertainment department are the lucky ones. The main reason is that those of us in the entertainment department don't have as many working hours as most of the other crew members. So, we have much more time to explore and enjoy the ship and the ports that the ship sails to. Most crew members working in the entertainment department have to work somewhere between four and six hours a day. Nearly all other crew members are working eight- to twelve-hour shifts. Some crew members, like the room stewards and security personnel, are sometimes working fourteen hours a day. Many of these crew members are only given a half-day off every week, and if they are unlucky enough to have their half-day off fall on a day when the ship is out at sea, then they only set foot on land for about four hours every two weeks. As a musician, I got off the ship at almost every port we sailed to. Sometimes, I didn't even get off the ship when we were in port simply because I had grown tired of the place after visiting it so many times. The point is that my experience was nothing like the experience of a crew member who has to sort garbage for twelve hours a day.

Therefore, it's extremely hard to answer the question "What is it like to work on a cruise ship?," because working on a cruise ship is different for every person who has ever set foot on these sailing cities. And every ship is different too. While all cruise ships share a common culture, each cruise ship on the seven seas is unique in the type of experience a crew member will have while working upon it. Every cruise ship has unique quirks, a unique milk schedule, and a distinctive onboard culture. The differences found when visiting two ships are similar to the differences you would find while visiting New York and L.A. These are both cities in America, but they are as different as they could possibly be.

The experience a crew member has on a cruise ship also greatly depends on what kind of attitude they take on board with them. Some people just don't belong out at sea, and they don't last. What it's like to work on a cruise ship also changes for crew members as time goes by. What it was like for me when I first started was nothing compared to what it was like five years later. I'll readily admit that the great attitude I had when I first started working on cruise ships faded fast. In the cruise ship show band, they call this "getting dark." I got dark, and you'll see why; but you'll also see why I stayed on the cruise ship for five years. When you first get onboard the cruise ship, it is a dream. But sometimes dreams fade. The most important thing is often the ability to recognize when your dream has turned into a nightmare and knowing when it is time to shake yourself awake and move on with your life. But for now, the ship was a dream. It was a dream come true, and it was time to live the dream. Everything has its time, and for now it was time to kick back, put the dial on cruise control, and enjoy the ride.

4

WHAT IS THE CREW AREA LIKE?

Below the waterline, under the sea, and in the deep depths of the behemoth, metal-clad ship is where the crew sleeps, lives, parties, and, most of all, works. The crew works. They toil, sweat, and work harder than you can imagine down there below the glossy railings, smooth wooden decks, glitz, glamour, and clean air of the passenger areas. One of the most remarkable aspects of a cruise ship is the pure number of man hours that are worked every day on a cruise. On your average-sized cruise ship, there are around 1,000 crew members who are mostly relegated to living a life completely under the waterline in the cramped quarters of the crew area. The overwhelming majority of these 1,000 crew members work no less than ten hours a day. Many of them work twelve to sixteen hours a day. It's true. This means every day, crew members work at least a combined 10,000 hours to make the cruise ship putter along towards Nassau, China, Bora Bora, or wherever it's headed—10,000 hours a day to make sure that 2,000 passengers can sit comfortably in the sun, sip that rum punch, eat that sizzling steak, and most importantly, do it all on a safe and (of course) well-painted ship.

This means that one crew member is working for five hours every day for each single passenger aboard every cruise ship. Most of this work, I mean a whopping 80 percent of it, is happening completely out of sight and out of mind of every passenger. It is happening concealed and tucked away beneath them, down in the crew area beneath their feet. Below passenger decks, and I mean way below the passenger decks, is where all of this work happens. Like a well-oiled machine, or the hive of a massive bee colony, or the center of a colossal ant mound, there are workers folding towels, cooking steaks, ordering more steaks, maintaining the engine, printing photos, perfecting dance moves, baking pastries, washing dishes, stacking bananas, shucking corn, counting money, practicing drums, and painting the same stairwell they painted yesterday. This constant toiling continues at every hour, day and night. The crew area is a place like no other, a place that closely resembles what you would imagine if you closed your eyes and envisioned a top-secret government outpost in a post-apocalyptic world where robots that look mostly like Southeast Asians run a massive industrial factory.

Even after five years working on a cruise ship, the smoothness in which the day-to-day operations were executed never ceased to amaze me. Imagine the highly complex and logistically astounding amount of activity that must happen in order to run a massive hotel. Now, put that hotel on a floating barge that has to cross oceans and rely on all sorts of extremely fickle navigation, mechanical, and culinary devices. Include the facts that you have to keep a tight schedule, get everyone home safely, get the crew paid on time, and can only restock your supplies once a week. Consider all of this together, and you start to get an idea of the kind of chaotic environment that the crew area can become. The chaos of the crew area is often heightened by an overwhelming sense of urgency. This is the type of environment that the crew must often work in, and this is a crew that is often underappreciated and almost always underpaid given the amount of bullshit that they have to put up with. And let me be clear here. I am not talking about myself. I was a musician. My life was pretty much easy sailing. I am talking about the Filipinos, the Indians, the Indonesians, the Russians, and that one Canadian guy with dreads I met that decided it was a good idea to become a pastry chef on the cruise ship and lasted an entire half a week. These are the crew members who deserve all the credit. These are the ones who work harder than a rice cook on a cruise ship and put up with more bullshit than a Montana cattle rancher.

The crew area can be a difficult place to live. The

most unbelievable aspect of the crew area is that many crew members have to stay down in that poorly lit, foul smelling, chaotic pit the entire time they are on the ship, except for the occasional times when there is a crew party on an open deck, and that is, unfortunately, not very often. However, the crew area is definitely not all bad. In fact, the best part of the crew area is that it is ours. It is the crew's area—a place where we can take a break from the passengers and hang out with people from our own city, people from the underground like us. Fellow crew members are the only other people on the ship who know what it is like to do what we do, and can laugh about all the funny and crazy things that happened on the ship yesterday and last night in the crew bar.

The crew area is where we can curse to the choir of fellow crew members who also understand the frustrations of working on a cruise ship— frustrations that can only be understood if you have done it, or have read this book, of course. This is where most of the cruise ship community gathers to work, but it is also where we gather to eat, celebrate, love, and play. It is our own little nook where we can get away and watch the sunrise crest over the sea without being asked directions to the Purser's Office, and where we can tuck into a warm bed and sleep for a few hours in absolute darkness with the sound of the merciless sea continuing its epic and never-ending battle with the side of the ship. It is a place where we can lift weights in our own tiny, foul-smelling gym and play our own odd mix of foreign dance music from all around the world. It is a place like no other, on a planet where the inhabitants are always moving forward, always going somewhere, and always have wind in their hair, but so much gel that it never blows or moves at all. It is a place where the ocean is always there to rock you to sleep, and where the soundtrack to life is more like the score to a Bollywood film than a Hollywood blockbuster (with a budget for the set to match). In the crew area, you can always find a good curry on the menu, no matter how many times you've told the chef you're tired of curry. And in the crew area, we cabin party like there's no tomorrow. It is a place that every crew member will cherish forever. The crew area embeds itself so deep into your mind that when you step into an old, rundown, two-star motel late at night, the stunning resemblance is enough to make you smile as you are filled with all the fond and distant memories of your adventurous life at sea.

So, let's take a quick tour of the crew area, shall we? If you're on a cruise right now, go and grab a map of the ship, preferably one of those maps that show the cruise ship sliced down the middle as a cross section diagram. If you aren't on a ship, I am sure you can find a map online or just use that nifty thing called your imagination. Take your map of the cruise ship, and draw a line just above deck five. Great. On most ships, nearly everything below that line is a crew area. Therefore, not the entire crew area is below the waterline, and thank God for that. If the crew had to spend their entire time in the crew area with only artificial light to fill their lives, it would be criminal at best. There are always other crew areas dotted here and there above deck five, and a lot of times the stairwells will be used as a staging area for food and drinks, so I guess they qualify as crew areas as well. Every little nook and cranny of the ship is used in some way or another. The commodity of space is extremely valuable on a ship. None of it is wasted. Not a single inch.

Since most of the crew area is below deck five on the majority of ships, this means there is only one single crew deck that is entirely above waterline, and also a deck that sits right at waterline which simply bobs in and out of the foamy sea. That is when the weather is good. When the weather is bad, you can see enormous waves splashing up against the tiny porthole windows. The other three or more decks of the crew area—depending on how big of a ship we're talking about—are completely submerged and windowless.

Thankfully, the crew bar is always above the waterline. And for most of the crew, the crew bar is the single most important room on a cruise ship. It rests high on a pedestal above all other crew areas, and its only competition, in a very distant second, is the crew deck. Some marine architects and designers of ships seem to be aware of this, and they have mercifully grouped them close to one another. There is nothing that comes close to the morale booster like a cruise ship that is designed so that a crew member can buy a one dollar Stella Artois, walk right from the crew bar out into the fresh air of the crew deck, let the sun hit their face for the first time in twelve hours as they tilt the bottom up and let some cold beer roll in, admire the fit and very hard working dancers in bikinis in the hot tub, and then join them for a soak as the ship cuts through the ocean while beautiful islands glide past like a private viewing of a *National Geographic* special. That is morale boosting at its absolute finest.

However, on many ships I have worked aboard, the crew bar is on the complete opposite end of the ship as the crew deck. I never thought that I would understand the reasoning behind this. That all changed one drunken night when I witnessed an absolutely tanked crew member take a full running start from the rail of the crew deck and leap into the empty crew pool. There was a loose net that was cast across the top of the pool and secured to small, metal hooks along the pool's edge. Apparently, he thought the rope netting would catch him, and he would bounce like a tightrope walker at a circus show. Have I mentioned that nearly everything on a ship is metal, from the ship's bell to the bottom of the crew pool? So, it was quite the circus show all right when the net collapsed under his weight, and his body bounced off of the metal bottom of the pool. We all expected to hear a thud, but the sound was more like a gong and the bells of Big Ben being struck together. It was both painful and hilarious to watch. The guy earned himself a trip to the medical center for a cast fitting and then a one-way ticket home when we landed in Long Beach, California the next day.

Yet, whether it is connected to the crew deck or not, the crew bar is the absolute favorite place of almost every crew member on the ship. As you can imagine, the crew bar is where the party happens. Well, the party at least starts in the crew bar. Then after the bar has closed, crew members pour out onto the crew deck and continue to party out there until security is called. Then the crew members move into the hallways and stairwells and eventually into someone's cabin until security is called again. Finally, the party is beaten to death at four in the morning. When I say party, I mean party. I will address this in more detail in Chapter 9 that is titled "What Is the Best Part About Working on a Cruise Ship?". However, let me reassure you that even though cruise ship crew members may not technically be sailors—I mean it's not like we're pulling the ropes, bringing in the lines, and battening down the hatches with parrots on our shoulders and wooden legs amongst us—the tradition of drinking like sailors and partying like pirates lives on in the crew bar. It lives on below the waterline.

The interior of the crew bar isn't much of anything to write home about, but I'll write about it anyway. There is often a short wooden bar that can barely fit eight people across, even though there are 1,000-and-something crew members that would like to get a drink on a Saturday night. And every night is Saturday night on the cruise ship. In fact, days and time have no meaning at all. You're either in port or you're not. It's either a port day or a sea day, and weekends, weekdays, Mondays, Sundays—they just don't exist. The only thing that exists is ship time, and ship time dictates the schedule of your life on the cruise ship. Ship time determines what time you work, what time you play, what time you eat, what time the crew bar opens, what time you can use the stage to practice drums, and what time they put out the new milk bag. You're on ship time. Cruise control. And the schedule for the rest of the world is totally irrelevant. You are completely, absolutely, for the first time in your life, untouchable by the GMT. You are untouchable by the world's time, and it feels great.

To be absolutely honest, the crew bar on a cruise ship usually looks like a rundown seafood restaurant— one of the kitschy ones that have those novel porthole windows and life preservers hanging on the walls. There is nothing remarkable or exceptional about the place. It's just a poorly lit bar with a snook table and a dart game going on at all hours of the night, surrounded by a mismatched collection of cheap tables, chairs, and swivel booths in severe need of reupholstering. All the furniture looks as if it was taken from a collection of different rooms, each room having an exceptionally different decorative direction. This is *exactly* what has happened. The crew bar is without exception the depository for unloved and unwanted cruise ship furniture, and no one gets turned around at the door to this orphanage for the four-wooden-legged children of the cruise ship world. All cruise ship furniture is finally put out to pasture in the crew bar after a lifetime of supporting the weight of millions of midnight buffet guzzling, cigar smoking, sunset watching, and bridge playing passengers. The crew bar is the indiscriminate nursing home for out of style furnishings.

At almost all hours in the crew bar, there is a

seemingly continuous Karaoke contest going on where the Filipinos are pouring their hearts out onto the vinyl floor while channeling a foreign version of Michael Bolton with very bad English. They sing with an intense passion to the greatest collection of love songs you've never heard of, as if they are auditioning for the next season of Filipino Idol. The crew bar may not be the nicest place to look at, but what it lacks in well-appointed elegance, it makes up for (ten-fold) in character. It's really a wonder that no one has made a reality TV show filmed entirely in the crew bar of a cruise ship. And if you're a TV producer out there reading this book, then call me. Let's do it. We'll make a million bucks.

In the center of the crew bar you will find a dance floor, at least on the ships big enough to have one. The dance floor is complete with all the spinning lights and disco balls of a real, albeit poorly-funded nightclub. There's never a cover in the crew bar, and the drinks are always cheap: one dollar and fifty cents for a shot, one fifty for a mixed drink, and one dollar for a beer. When you don't have anything else to really spend your money on, a night at the crew bar can devolve very quickly into a very fun situation.

Like I said earlier, the second best destination in the crew area is the crew deck, and it rocks (whether it is connected to the crew bar or not). It more than rocks, in fact, the crew deck is undeniably and absolutely vital to the sanity and well-being of the crew. The crew deck is usually in the front of the ship. If you are on a cruise ship right now and you want to see the crew deck, go and find the lowest open-air passenger deck on the front of the ship. Walk out to the railing and look down. Usually, the crew deck will be right below you. There is often a hot tub and it is usually not working. There is also often a pool that is similar in size to a child's wading pool. Apparently, the cruise companies feel this is an adequate size to accommodate more than 1,000 crew members. When the pools and hot tubs on the crew deck are not drained and covered with nets— that for the record are not anything like trampolines or circus nets—they are the perfect place to sit, relax, and watch the sunset.

Unfortunately, this is not usually possible. Like most nice amenities that are provided for the crew on a cruise ship, the pools and hot tubs on the crew deck are usually either inaccessible or permanently broken. Cruise companies seem to have a real penchant for neglecting crew facilities. The passengers' saunas, steam rooms, pools and hot tubs are nearly always fully operational, every hour of every day on every cruise. However, if my observations of waterless hot tubs and pools are any indication, the crew area hot tubs and pools are the last on the list to get fixed. For example, I was on a cruise in Alaska for two months. The crew hot tub was broken the entire time. And I can't think of a more appropriate and enjoyable time to have a crew hot tub than when you are sailing through Alaska's inside passage with brisk blue-sky days and surrounded by rugged snowcapped mountains. I had a fantasy of sipping my morning coffee in that hot tub that was never fulfilled, and I will never let the cruise company live it down. There is no reason to neglect the crew hot tubs, especially at a time like that.

At night, the crew deck can be a wonderful thing. On some long voyages, when the ship is out in open water and the hour is late, the captain will often turn off the lights around the bridge so that he and his officers can more clearly see the faint glows of buoys and the lights of smaller watercraft that are also on the sea. This is when the stars come out. This is when the crew comes out as well. The crew drifts out onto the open deck to see the heavens above and to watch them glitter in the darkest skies they have ever seen. This is when we would emerge from the pounding dance music of the crew bar and be amazed at the sight in the skies on the other side of that big metal door. We would spend hours lying on our backs, listening to the waves of the sea crash against the side of the ship, and listening to the hypnotic moaning of metal cables stretched tight by the weight of the cruise liner as it pierced through the ocean and cut through the darkness of the Caribbean night. We were amazed by the sky like school children again as the ship crested wave after wave, sending us soaring up towards the stars and then falling once again towards the sea—the only living things separating the ocean from the dazzling night sky. It was magical.

The crew deck was where we watched city after city, all around the world, come into view and then tower around us as we tied up to docks from St. Thomas to Shanghai. It was the best seat in the house for sunset sails through the Philippine Islands and under Australia's Sydney Bridge as we sailed past the Sydney Opera House. It was where the crew could take long deep breaths full of fresh, crisp, clean air—a highly prized commodity for the crew. It was the best place to watch dolphins ride the waves pushed from the side of the ship, and the perfect place to stand on the ship's bow and pretend to be Jack from the movie *Titanic*. We would run up to the front of the ship, throw our arms out as wide as they could go, and yell as loud as possible, "I'm the king of the world!", and we sure felt like it. It was the perfect place to think. The crew deck was the perfect place to be, looking out over the ocean searching the horizon for what was coming next. And the best part was that there was always something coming next. We were always going somewhere. We were always in motion, and the crew deck was the front row seat. It was the first place you would find out what was just beyond the horizon of the sea, and far-away beyond the ship in the galaxy far above.

Now let's continue along on our tour. Next to the crew bar is where you usually find the crew Internet room—the crew's lifeline to the outside world. Before most of the ships at sea had wireless Internet for the crew to use, the crew Internet room was the only place you could get Internet access and send emails to family and friends, and to transfer money and pay bills back home. Unfortunately, Internet access on a ship is insanely, unbelievably, frighteningly expensive. There is probably no other reason than greed that can explain why cruise companies want to bilk their already low paid crew members out of their hard earned money and charge more than ten cents a minute to use the Internet. I mean, these are companies that are already probably making billions in profits, and they are choosing to charge their own employees twenty dollars for 200 minutes of Internet time. Many of these crew members are paid little more than $300 a week for more than sixty hours of work. One Internet card for just 200 minutes of time costs many crew members 10 percent of their weekly wage, and crew members spend it. They don't have much of a choice.

If I stacked up all of the little plastic Internet cards that I bought over the five year period I worked on cruise ships, the stack would probably stand higher than a two-story house. If you stacked up all the internet cards that have been purchased by every crew member since the cruise companies started selling these damn things, the stack would probably stretch to the moon and back. And each one of these Internet cards cost a crew member twenty hard-earned dollars. Crew members get paid one day, and then the next they put an endless stream of twenty dollar bills right back into company pockets, over-paying for plastic cards with Internet access codes on them. If you thought the coal mine company-store days were over, think again. It just goes to prove that you can't ever completely eradicate an immensely greedy idea. This may be price gouging. It is definitely tacky. Some may say it is reprehensible and unscrupulous, and I would agree with them. Give the crew free Internet! This is the least cruise companies can do for the people who are working their asses off for them. Besides, if you are a passenger right now, look at how much the cruise line is charging *you* to access the Internet. Don't you think the cruise line is already making enough money off of you and the other passengers to make at least a decent profit from their Internet service? Do you think they really need to make money off the crew as well?

Nowadays, the crew Internet rooms are much quieter. However, crew members are spending more money than ever on those Internet cards. This is because they can access the Internet in their crew cabins now. Crew members can now access the Internet from practically anywhere on the ship, 24/7. Many of you may feel that I am exaggerating. Many of you may still think 200 minutes of internet time for twenty dollars is not such a bad deal. If you think 200 minutes is a lot of Internet time, you have to understand that the Internet on a ship is dreadfully, embarrassingly, pull-your-hair-out, frustratingly slow. This isn't the same Internet you find on land. This isn't the Internet you know and love. This Internet is not high speed. It probably is not transmitted through cable or across cell towers. This is 1990s slow. This is dial-up speed Internet. And when the cruise companies have crew members paying ten cents a minute, it may be reasonable to assume that the cruise companies don't have much reason or motivation to try and improve the speed of their Internet systems. It's beyond frustrating. It's beyond a rip-off. Unfortunately, I don't believe it will change any time soon. Then again, there are those nifty little comment cards that all of you passengers can fill out.

Now, let's move on. As you would probably imagine, a large section of the crew area is taken up by crew cabins, food and beverage storage rooms, officers' cabins, crew offices, and the engine control room. Occasionally, the ship offers tours of the engine room, and it is well worth the time if you are at all interested by machinery and how things work. The enormous size of the ship's machinery is astounding. It is breathtaking to stand in the room where the anchor cable is wound onto a giant wench that is larger than you can imagine. The engine room is really worth seeing. You can ask at the Purser's desk if the ship you are on is offering tours during your cruise.

The engine room is also notable because it is loud. Very loud. I know this first-hand because I have had the unfortunate luck and absolute displeasure to have a room not only right next to the engine room, but also right next to each and every one of the other loudest rooms on a ship. Once, I shared a room with another unfortunate crew member. We woke up every morning, sometimes as bright and early as 7 o'clock, to the sound of crew members enthusiastically using chisels and hammers to chip paint off of hollow metal rails. Apart from the fact that it drove us to the brink of insanity as a result of chronic sleep deprivation, it was the most effective alarm clock I have ever owned. The painting on a ship never stops, and so the chipping of paint never ends either. I've spent time living in crew cabins that were only separated by a thin wall from the giant mechanical spool that winches the metal cable for the anchor into a nice bundle. The wall to my cabin would violently vibrate every time the metal cable was being wrapped around the winch. I've had cabins near the engine room where the hum of the engine never seemed to stop, and the level of noise coming from that room never ceased to amaze me. I've lived in rooms across the hall from heavy metal doors that every crew member seemed to use, and every time they were opened they would clang shut in an eruption of noise that sounded like someone was dropping a cast iron tub full of pots and pans into the Grand Canyon. The first room I lived in on the *Fantasy*, and many of the rooms afterward, were regrettably positioned just below a hallway where it sounded like someone was dragging an odd assortment of heavy chains, or rehearsing a version of *A Christmas Carol* three times a day, where the only section acted out was when Jacob Marley, the ghost of Christmas past, came to town. The ship can be a very loud place if you have a room in the wrong spot, and I am sorry to report to you that there are an exceptionally high number of very wrong spots in which you can have a room on a cruise ship.

Like the crew deck, the crew mess is usually near the crew bar, clustered in the back or front of the ship with all the other places that the crew favors. Actually, there are four different dining halls. Each rank of crew members among the ship's hierarchy has their own dining hall where they can consume their three square meals with those of similar ilk. This means that the crew, the staff, the officers, and the captain all eat in separate areas. This is a testament to the extreme and overwhelmingly distasteful stratification that exists on a ship. As you go down the hierarchy, each dining hall offers a progressively worse experience. The captain is at the top of this hierarchy. He has his own dining room, a nice long wooden table, a group of servers to take his order and pour his wine. At the very bottom of this hierarchy is the crew mess. And as we shall see, it is truly a mess.

I had the opportunity to dine with the captain in the captain's dining room. I was picked to be an employee of the month. As a result, I received an extra hundred bucks, a special nametag that did little more than induce ridicule from the other crew members, my photo on the I-95 (even more ridicule inducing than the nametag), and the chance to finally eat some decent food with the captain. It turned out to be quite the odd affair. It was fascinating, for sure, and very enjoyable to say the least. The food was certainly of better quality than what they were feeding those of us on the staff, and it goes without saying that the food the captain was dining on was of infinitely better quality than what the crew is served. Eating at the captain's table was a real treat. It was like finally getting to use your reservation at the French Laundry after eating nothing but Hardee's for six months straight. No, Hardee's is better than the food served in a cruise ship crew mess.

The irony of the whole situation is that the crew, the passengers, the staff, the captain, and the officers are all surrounded by the best food money can buy. I mean, one of the most magnetically attractive qualities of a cruise ship is the fact that it is a giant floating meal-machine. A cruise ship is a sailing buffet and casino headed to exotic places with beautiful beaches where you can experience something different than what you experience every other day of your life at home. Crew members are surrounded, literally surrounded day and night, by an unimaginable mountain of culinary delicacies. And it is the crew (not the staff or the officers, in my opinion) who work the hardest out of everyone on the cruise ships. The crew labors day and night to keep this unstoppable river of food flowing. Yet, the crew is given the dregs of the ship's food supply. They are offered the bottom of the barrel and treated as if they are bottom-feeders. Having to eat in the crew mess is like being surrounded by water with nothing to drink, except you have something to drink, but it doesn't look or taste very good, and you've been drinking it for eight months straight, and you were absolutely sick of it seven months ago. I'm telling you, the tradition of hard tack lives on aboard these ships. It lives on in the form of low quality lentil curry and pork knuckle stew.

Therefore, getting to eat with the captain was a *big* deal. Getting to eat a really well-cooked meal that hasn't been sitting under a heat lamp for six hours and wasn't prepared in a giant pot in a portion that could feed my entire hometown was a big deal. Getting to sit and have dinner with the most important man on the ship and being able to look out at the sea through brass bordered portholes while we ate steaks and drank endless cups of wine from real glasses was inspiring, and a really big deal. On a cruise ship, getting to do anything other than what you have to do every single day over and over again is a really big deal.

I was hoping to hear stories from the captain of how he wrestled giant squid from the bow of his shrimp boat before he became captain of the cruise ship, or how he battled pirates off the coast of Somalia while he worked as the captain of a cargo freighter before retiring to the luxury of navigating this gargantuan pleasure craft—but no such luck. The captain was interested in us. Before the night was over, and after many glasses of the best red wine you can find on a cruise ship without actually going into a passenger area, we were all laughing and singing. And I mean literally singing some random Indonesian folk songs that a few of the other employees-of-the-month taught us after our fifth bottle or so.

However, there usually isn't much singing in the crew mess. The most common sound is CNN ranting on about some conflict in the Middle East or the latest soccer match that is going on in the world. The crew mess is simply a large hall that is outfitted with more old tables and chairs, lit by fluorescent lighting, and designed with as little color as possible, apparently by the same people who designed every other crew area on a cruise ship. These people either really love the color tan, or it is the cheapest color paint you can buy, because nearly everything in the crew area is tan—the floors, the walls, the tables, the chairs. They are all mostly a dull and boring color tan.

One thing the crew mess has going for it is that there is a considerably large selection of food on the crew mess buffet. There are a few meats maybe, always a fish selection, plenty of curries, a fish-head stew or two, hot dogs, rice, rice, and more rice, yoghurt, a few deserts of a strange gelatin consistency, and the three staples that most crew members live off of—Raisin Bran, Cheerios, and Corn Flake cereals. The problem isn't the variety. The problem is that it is always the same variety, and after a few months you are sick of it; I mean, can't-bring-the-fork-to-your-mouth-without-gagging sick of it.

Fortunately, musicians are considered staff members, and staff members have their own dining hall that is connected to the crew mess. The staff mess is in a separate, much quieter, and cleaner room. Staff members and officers have waiters. On most ships, staff members and officers can also order off a menu that includes several of the meal choices that passengers are served in the guest dining rooms. Best of all, on many cruise ships, officers and staff members can drink free white or red wine with meals. Because of this, musicians and other staff members spend a lot of time in the staff mess. Some of my fondest memories of working on a cruise ship consist of sitting with my musician friends for hours in the staff mess where we would laugh, tell jokes, and vent our frustrations while I sipped my fifth cappuccino and polished off my third apple crumble desert after eating two plates of mashed potatoes, filet mignon, a healthy serving of French fries, and after drinking a few (OK, maybe more than a few) glasses of wine.

The funny thing is that crew members even get tired of *that*. I got tired of the filet mignon because it was the same filet mignon I had been eating for six months. Even though I could have filet mignon for free on the ship, I actually found myself buying it in port just to get different filet mignon. It's crazy, and I suspect I won't be getting any sympathy from the peanut gallery, but it's frighteningly true. The cruise ship teaches many things, and one is that you can get tired of anything no matter how good it is—even free filet mignon. Somehow, being on a cruise ship seems to just speed up this process of getting tired of things. It is a getting-tired-of-things accelerator, and it is set to high speed.

Next to the staff mess is the officers' dining hall, but I'm not allowed in there as a staff member, so I don't know anything about it. All I know is what I've seen from the threshold that separates the chosen from the common staff folk. I have seen the white table cloths, the steaming plates of better prepared meals, a larger menu, a wait staff that can actually speak English, and meals delivered in less than 30 minutes (and that's saying a lot when compared to a cruise ship staff mess). To a staff or crew member, the officers' mess looks like cruise ship dining hall heaven. It looks like the place where all the good, hard working, talented, or otherwise butt-kissing staff members go after they die and become cruise directors, officers, staff captains, and payroll managers.

Interestingly, I have known quite a few staff members who will not eat in the staff mess. They will only eat in the crew mess with the rest of the crew. They do this in protest of the stratified nature of the ship. I guess it is the closest thing to a hunger strike while still eating—a symbolic gesture of poor food subjection to show respect for the masses of the less fortunate. I was never so boldly altruistic or revolutionarily spirited in my dining hall choices, but I nonetheless felt sorry for the crew who never got to order off a menu, order decent coffee, or get tired of filet mignon (because you haven't lived until you have become tired of filet mignon). I felt sorry for the crew who never got to order free wine, or had the opportunity to be waited on by people who cannot understand what you are trying to order because they can speak and understand as much English as a deaf elephant. The crew seemed to live mostly off mountains of steaming rice (good God, I've never seen so much rice on one plate in my life). And while I don't know what it is like to ingest more rice than is probably safe for one human body during a single meal, I did feel their pain. I did wish that things were not the way they were. Unfortunately, they are most likely still this way. It just didn't feel right. It doesn't feel right writing about it either. I feel like I should have done more to be supportive towards the crew. If I ever go on a cruise ship I will just have to make up for it and make sure to tip them well.

While I could go on about this forever (oh, wait, I already did) I should move this uncensored tour right along, and take you into the real heart of the ship— the crew office. Like a heart, none of the crew members would be on the cruise ship if the crew office didn't exist, because the crew office is where all the crew members get paid. It is usually located mid-ship just off the I-95, the main thoroughfare for foot traffic—that big hallway just at waterline that stretches from one end of the ship to the other. It is amazing the type of bookkeeping that must take place on a cruise ship. I am fortunate enough to have never had the displeasure of knowing this painstaking and taken-for-granted job. I can imagine that money is flowing everywhere on a cruise ship, and it would be one heck of a job to keep track of it all. In all the years I worked on cruise ships, not once (well maybe once or twice) was I paid late. A ship is a place where punctuality is a necessity. The ship has to get into port on time. Therefore, everything else has to run on time too. The itinerary is sacred. This way of thinking migrates from the captain all the way down to the crew. For the band, it is felt in the fact that the show must go on, and it must go on at exactly 7 o'clock p.m. On the dot. No questions asked.

Everyone is paid on time as a result of this meticulous clock-watching religion that you must conform to aboard the cruise ship. Unfortunately, all crew members are usually paid at the same exact time, on the same day, from the same single person sitting behind a single window dispensing checks like they were selling tacos from a taco truck in northern California. And this is one hell of a popular taco truck. The line can stretch thirty people long, and if you want your check, you have to wait in line.

Now let's continue to walk down the I-95. All along this main hallway you will find an enormous variety of food storage rooms and food preparation facilities. In one room there are crew members wearing aprons smeared with blood. They are carving tenderloins, slicing steaks, and trimming roasts at all hours of the day. In another room, there are crew members whose single objective is to slice vegetables for 10 hours a day or so. These crew members robotically feed endless supplies of green peppers, tomatoes, onions, and potatoes into the spinning silver blades of the mechanical slicers. The vegetables are sorted into individual and colorful piles like the choices of paint on a painter's palette, and these piles reach to the ceiling and fill the room.

At the end of the I-95, you reach the front of the ship and a stairwell that often leads down to the ship's main laundry facility. Think of every person on an entire cruise ship—all 2,000-plus passengers, and 1,000-plus crew members. Think of how many towels, sheets, blankets, and pillow cases they all use every single day. I know when I was working on the ship, I would use about two towels a day, and I wasn't going to the pool two or three times a day like most passengers do. Every day, these tens of thousands of sheets, towels, and pillow cases must be washed and then taken down to the ship's main laundry room at bottom of the ship.

The ship's main laundry is truly an astounding site. The entire bottom of the ship is filled with washing machines and dryers, industrial-sized soaking tanks, and massive spinning machines that can hold hundreds of sheets or towels at a time. All of the clean laundry is then funneled into a single room where unseen and unheard crew members endlessly toil.

These crew members stack, fold, and deliver an unfathomable amount of laundry to every corner of the sailing city. The laundry facility is a well-oiled machine that is practically flawless in ensuring that passengers and crew members are always provided with linens that are perfectly white and clean. As an example, I would go to the gym nearly every day when I worked on the cruise ship. Not once was there a shortage of towels. I would put my hand out to grab a towel and a perfectly clean stack of towels was always there, and they were always neatly rolled or stacked. It is easy to overlook how much work goes into a single cruise. It is especially easy to have stacks of towels go unnoticed and unappreciated. However, there is an exceptional amount of work behind these stacks of towels. And if you are on a cruise right now, let's do what I call "The Towel Test." Stop anywhere on the ship and ask a crew member for a towel. I would put money on it that there is a stack of towels within a few hundred feet from where you are standing. I guarantee that you will have a towel in your hand within the next five minutes, and often the towel will not just be folded into a boring old square. It will be folded into the shape of a monkey or a dolphin or a detailed miniature replication of Buckingham Palace complete with a hand towel that was folded to resemble the Queen of England having her afternoon tea inside of the palace or something. It is astounding what these crew members do.

It is also astounding what the crew members' personal laundry facility looks like. The passengers' laundry facility is consistently and reliably humming away. The laundry machines are sparkling clean. No passenger will ever go a minute without a clean towel. However, the same crew members who work so hard to make this possible have to fight it out below the waterline for the opportunity to use one of the rusted, dented, duct-taped, rattling, barely working, poor excuse for a washer or dryer found in the crew laundry room. That's if they can even find a washer or dryer that works.

The crew laundry room is a truly unbelievable and pathetic sight. It is usually located just above the main laundry near the front of the ship. Crew members find so much duct tape on the half-dead laundry machines in the crew laundry that they think duct tape was invented for this purpose. I'm not going to get into all the strangeness that surrounds these twenty machines and the battles that go on to secure a prized position in the crew laundry waiting game, but I will say that one of the best parts of living on land is living life without having to share the world's smallest and most poorly maintained community Laundromat with 1,000 other people.

The crew laundry is an absurdity. First, there are more than a thousand crew members and usually only around twenty machines. Secondly, most of the crew hardly has the time to clean their clothes. Thirdly, the facility does not aptly meet the definition of a laundry room. This is much too strong of a name for the place, as it implies that this is a facility where you are actually able to go wash and dry your clothes. It should be called the "crew room to get rust in your clothes and half dried because none of the machines fucking work properly facility." It is pathetic. It should induce some form of shame and indignity in every executive who has ever worked for a cruise line with facilities for their crew as unacceptable and unfitting as this. Of course, officers have their own laundry room. The machines there work. They are sparkling. There is no duct tape to be found, and officers only have to share their laundry facility with a hundred other people or so. It is hierarchical bullshit at its finest. We are all human on a cruise ship. Just like officers, crew members deserve the ability to clean the sweat and blood and dried hair gel out of their clothes so they can at least continue to bust their asses in a clean shirt and trousers.

If you're on a cruise right now and you smell a crew member with extremely offensive body odor (and I guarantee you will), don't go to the Purser's Office and complain about that crew member. Go to the Captain at the Captain's Cocktail and complain about the crew laundry room. Tell him Josh Kinser sent you. He'll know who I am. I complained to him about the conditions of the crew laundry room. I talked to every captain on every ship I was aboard. And all of them did absolutely nothing about it. And why would they? The captain probably has his own laundry room. Like I said before, it's absolute pretentious snobbery. It's hierarchical bullshit at its finest. Give the crew the ability to wash their clothes.

Surrounding all of these areas I have described, and filling every possible nook of the ship, is a maze of the tiniest crew cabins you can imagine. Crew members are packed two to a room and often four or more crew members must share one single bathroom. Spartan is an understatement when it comes to describing the crew cabins. There is a bunk bed in the back of the room, a desk to one side against the wall, and a wardrobe against the other wall. If a crew member brings more than two chairs into his or her cabin, this is often enough to make the room exceptionally crowded.

But, it is a ship, after all, and crew members make it work. Actually, we do more than make it work; we make it fun. If you go to a crew cabin after about ten at night, you will often find ten or more crew members all crammed next to each other. Most of the time, you will find them smiling, laughing, and celebrating ship life. This is because even though there is a very frustrating side to working on cruise ships, most crew members are happy to be working out at sea. They are happy to be floating for a while in the ocean. They are pleased to put real life on hold for a minute and tap their lives back into cruise control where they can just ride the waves, do their jobs, get tired of filet mignon, drink their free wine, look out of their porthole windows (if you are an officer) from their tiny little crew cabins (if you are not an officer), and worry about nothing else but where the sea is going to take them next. The crew area may be shabby and cramped for the most part, but the crew area is not the most dominant feature of a crew member's life. The crew area is merely where we live. Ship life is what we experience, and ship life can be a beautiful thing.

And now we have come to the end of our tour of the crew area. I hope you have enjoyed it. And I think this would be the appropriate place to say thank you to all of the hard working crew members who make all of these wonderful cruises possible. This would be the appropriate place to say bravo, well done. We all, passengers and staff and officers included, could not have done it and continue to do it without you. Thanks.

And if you are on a cruise right now and there has been a waiter, or a room steward, or an officer, or (and I know this is a stretch) a drummer in the show band that has made your cruise exceptionally enjoyable, I encourage you to pull them aside and say thank you. I encourage you to let them know how much you appreciate all the work that they do so that you can enjoy your cruise. As a crew member, I know how rare it is for a passenger to say this, and I know how much of a difference it can make in the life of a crew member. We often live in a compassionless world, but we have the ability to transform a cruise ship into the world that we wish we had. We all go on a cruise to escape from real life. Taking a cruise is like a fantasy. So, let's also take a break from how ruthlessly we usually treat one another and make the fantasy of taking a cruise a little more fantastic.

And if you are on a cruise right now, have taken one in the past, or are planning one as we speak, I want to say thank you. You and every other passenger make ship life possible for every crew member, and I sincerely thank you for the opportunity to experience what it is like to live and work aboard a cruise ship.

And if there is a crew member that has made your cruise exceptionally memorable and enjoyable, I encourage you to tip them, and tip them well. Many of these crew members have wages so low and come from countries with such poor economies, that an extra twenty dollars can make a huge difference in their lives. Tip them, and tip them well; especially the Indians, Filipinos, and the Indonesians. Believe me—they deserve it.

5

WHAT IS IT LIKE TO WORK AS A MUSICIAN ON A CRUISE SHIP?

Playing music aboard a cruise ship is extremely different than playing music on land. The biggest change is that you don't feel the anxiety from not knowing where the next gig is going to come from. For the most part, musicians are nervous, neurotic, spastic, hyper, and frantic people. It's not just the music that does this to us. Part of it is not knowing where you're going to find that next gig. Part of it is always having to beat the pavement, always having to be out in the fray, always living out in the heart of the hustle. It's exciting. You feel alive when you are always living on the edge and always know that a big break into the major leagues of the music business could be just around the corner. There's not much that motivates and excites you more than being on the edge of massive possibilities. This is where musicians live their lives. It is like living at the base camp to Mount Everest in more ways than one. You have a shit load of gear to carry around with you, and you have to live off ramen noodles and trail mix until you have the chance to see what the world looks like from a higher vantage point.

I believe that people choose to become musicians mostly because they can't live without creating music. These are people who have a deep passion and love for creating things. And thankfully they are creating music. If they weren't creating music they would most likely be creating children that most of them cannot afford. I also believe that people who become musicians do it because they crave to exist as close as they can to those great big possibilities. The hustle is exceptionally invigorating. It is a lot of fun too. And creating something new and fresh every day, prying it right out of your imagination and drive, is unexplainably exciting, rewarding, energizing, and stimulating. It can also be incredibly exhausting.

Fortunately, the hustle is not allowed to board the cruise ship. The hustle was left standing on the dock with suitcases packed and ready to go. The suitcases were stuffed full of hard work and sweat. They were bursting at the seams with flyers for bar gigs with five dollar cover charges, business cards, massive phone bills, gas bills for the band van, and the wood chips of a thousand chewed-up drumsticks. The hustle is not welcomed on the cruise ship. And at the time, I didn't mind seeing it take a temporary hiatus.

On my second day aboard the cruise ship, we were pulling into Nassau. This was the first stop on a long adventure of ports that would stretch over five years. I had lived my whole life in Florida. I had never been closer to the Caribbean than the outer edges of the Everglades on a canoe trip. I was bouncing with excitement about seeing my first island in the Bahamas. Then I was told that I wasn't going anywhere. I had a special reservation to attend new employee training, and the training was going to last the next four days. That's right. New crew members must endure four straight days of the worst corporate training videos (probably produced around 1980) that you will ever watch in your entire life. The acting in these videos is worse than what you find in the first-aid training films at an American Red Cross certification program, and that's saying something.

It turned out I wasn't going to be seeing *any* of the ports on my first cruise at all. In fact, while the ship docked alongside countless palm-tree-shaded beaches with rum bars, bikinis, and tiki torches that faded into a misty horizon, I was going to be in yet another completely tan colored room memorizing how to use a fire extinguisher and where all the muster stations are located across the entire ship. This was apparently just in case my drum set spontaneously burst into flames or something. My first cruise was going to be a *wash*. I would spend it in a tiny room, listening to some corporate drone recite the same environmental regulations and safety policies he had been reciting to the endless flow of new employees for the past thirty-five years. I listened to the corporate trainer with as much focus and interest as Lindsay Lohan at a court proceeding; his voice bore a shocking resemblance to Charlie Brown's teacher (wah-wah, wah-wah-wah-wah). I stared out the window as fellow crew members filed down the gangway wearing sleeveless shirts, sunglasses, flip-flops, and gel in their hair (yes, even to the beach do crew members wear gel in their hair). The crew members were headed to some tropical paradise where women played beach volleyball topless or something.

The training was the pits. I went through that entire medical evaluation fiasco just to spend another four days trapped in corporate, liability-risk-reduction hell; and it was a completely tan-colored hell that smelled like paint fumes, to boot. I went and poured myself a big glass of the best free milk on the planet. Then I sulked for a while, holding my neon colored plastic cup in my new-employee hands. The trainer dimmed the lights and pressed play for the worst training videos ever produced in all the history of mankind. At that moment, in the darkness of that training room, I was initiated. I had officially become a proper cruise ship crew member. There was no turning back now.

After five hours, the training was finally over for the day. I had a chance to eat very quickly, and then I had to run across the ship to a rehearsal with the band in The Cat's Meow. The bags of cat food on the wall and the dance floor that looked like a fake tire were actually starting to grow on me somehow. I was beginning to embrace the fact that this was our stage and that this was our club. I decided that I had better start taking some pride in The Cat's Meow, no matter how ridiculous and repulsive the lounge really looked.

Over the next week we performed so well that we packed the club every night. I began to get to know some of the other crew members and really started to dig the whole flow of the schedule. I would get up in the morning and have breakfast at the crew mess. Then I would go to corporate training hell, a productive rehearsal, a short break, and then it was time for the nightly performance in The Cat's Meow. The night usually ended at the crew bar. I was making friends with some of the other musicians, and more importantly I was meeting some of the stunningly beautiful female dancers on the ship. Occasionally, the dancers would come by on their nights off or in between shows and listen to us play. Sometimes they would get on stage and sing with the band. It is a little known fact that most dancers are wonderful singers as well. It is just a part of their training. We all know that cruise ship dancers are the most beautiful creatures to have ever set foot on this earth. Top that with a healthy dose of charm and the talents of dancing and singing, and you have an irresistibly perfect recipe for falling in love.

When I had the chance, I would take a minute or two during the breaks of our performances and run over to the main theater to watch a bit of the production shows. I really liked what I saw. The musicians were top notch. They were reading charts and playing all styles of music that included traditional jazz, Latin music, Motown, and rock. It was phenomenal! The orchestra was backing up the dancers and a group of incredible singers. *That would be fun to do one day, if I could read good enough,* I thought. But for now, I was a club drummer, and I was playing by ear.

Many people probably don't realize that there is a big difference between reading charts and playing music by ear. Some musicians can't read a lick of written music, including many greatly revered musicians. I grew up just listening to music and playing what I heard. This is considered learning to play by ear. When you learn an instrument by ear you are exploring your own ideas and exploring the sounds of an instrument without any preconceived direction, roadmap, or constructs that tell you what you can or cannot play. I believe that learning an instrument by ear really helps a musician tap into the ability to play what they hear in their head. Playing by ear seems to help a musician express what they feel and strengthens their ability to tap into those feelings. It also seems to improve their ability to improvise on their instrument. This is just as important on a drum set as it is on other instruments. Playing by ear is also a wonderful way to learn the vocabulary of an instrument—all the sounds an instrument can really make. However, learning to read music allows a musician to access the written ideas of musicians from all time. Reading music usually helps a musician to refine technique. It can also reveal a great deal about the traditional or conventional approaches to most musical genres.

The first time I saw the show band play, it made me want to really learn how to read music. I could see these huge folders that were stuffed full of music charts and sitting on the music stands. I knew how to read music a little. I had worked with the jazz bands and symphonic groups in college, but I wanted to be able to look at a page of music and know what it said like I was reading a book. I wanted to be able to read music without any effort and interpret the music in my own way like the show band guys were able to do. It was inspiring.

For a musician, the amount of inspiration that can be found on a ship is one of the best parts of working on a cruise ship. There are musicians on the lido deck for five hours a day pumping out authentic roots-driven reggae and calypso. These are sounds of the Caribbean performed by people who have lived it and breathed it all of their lives. There are the jazz cats in the orchestra that are fresh out of the top music schools like Berkeley, Texas A&M, and Julliard. Then you have the jazz trio guys who are completely immersed in jazz and want to play nothing more than slow ballads by Miles Davis and out-there bop compositions by Thelonious Monk. Then you have us pop junkies in the lounge band performing Motown, rock, funk, and modern dance tunes. In the band that I performed with on the cruise ship, I don't think one of us held a degree in music. I don't think any of us were able to read music very well either. We were just playing music by ear and expressing how we felt. And an incredible aspect of working as a musician on the ship is that once you get to know all of the different musicians, they usually welcome you to stop by their performances and play music with them. I remember walking out on the lido deck during a break from a performance in The Cat's Meow, and the Jamaican guys in the reggae band were playing "Red Red Wine". They changed the lyrics to *Josh Josh Josh. Come play a song with us.* I jumped up on stage and grooved for a few minutes to Bob Marley's "One Love" before heading back to The Cat's Meow to finish my performance there.

The same can be said about the other musicians on the ship. I would sometimes head over to the cigar bar and sit in with the jazz trio. I would try out my best *spang-a-lang, spang-a-lang* on the ride cymbal or my newest jazz licks before heading to the crew bar. It is a very inspiring place to work as a young musician who is extremely interested in exploring music. It is a real treat to have access to so many stages that feature such a rich diversity of musical styles. The cruise ship is a great place to learn how to play and perform music. I definitely recommend it to anyone who is having a hard time finding a gig right now.

Another thing I learned on the cruise ship is that there are a lot of rules to follow out at sea. I didn't know any of the rules on the ship when I first started working there. There are many petty rules on a cruise ship and so many unreasonable people trying to enforce them. These insignificant rules can choke the fun right out of the job. They often turn what could be the most enjoyable place to live into a nearly unlivable environment. However, when I first climbed aboard the cruise ship, I was living on a cruise ship with no rules. I was walking in a wonderful type of blissful ignorance, completely unaware that I was breaking thousands of rules on a daily basis. It was a blast.

The best example of this occurred during my first week aboard the ship. A pretty girl walked into The Cat's Meow. She was wearing brown leather boots, a white backless shirt, and she danced all night. We ended up hanging out after my last set. We were having a few drinks, talking, and laughing when she asked me if she could see the crew area. *Why the hell not?* I thought. *This was a cruise ship without rules, right?* I would later find out that I was about to break one of the top three rules for a cruise ship crew member:

1) Under no circumstances is a crew member permitted to have sex with a passenger.

2) Do not at any time bring an unauthorized passenger into a crew area.

3) Do not bring drugs aboard the cruise ship or use any illegal substances while working as a cruise ship crew member.

These are the big three, and if you break these rules you will be fired and sent home immediately. No questions asked. No ticket home. Nonetheless, these rules are broken nearly every day.

I didn't know these rules yet, so I brought her down to the crew area. I took her straight to the crew deck and right to the bow of the ship. I didn't realize at the time that the crew deck is directly below the bridge where all the officers and the captain of the ship work. From the bridge, the officers and the captain have an aerial view of the crew deck. I took her right out to the front of the ship, right below the bridge, and she immediately climbed onto the top rail at the edge of the deck. We are racing through the ocean. The wind is whipping her hair and her dress in all directions. She looks at me and laughs because she can see that I am more concerned about her safety than she is. The ship is charging through waves. She loosely wraps her legs around the rail of the ship to keep herself from falling overboard and being sucked into the ship propellers. She smiles. I try to convince her to come down, but she's having way too much fun. I'm eyeing the life preserver attached to the front of the ship and figuring out in my head the best way to unravel the tightly wound rope in case I have to act at a moment's notice. She's laughing her ass off. Suddenly, a bright spot light targets right onto her face. The light is beaming down from up in the bridge. A voice comes over the loudspeaker.

"Get down-ah from the rail of the ship-ah!"

She curls her lip and gives me this exaggerated look like a baby when you take away its bottle. All her fun is spoiled. She slowly slides off the rail and back onto the safety of the deck. The next day I told some of the guys in the band the story. They told me I would no longer be a cruise ship musician if the captain or any of the officers had known I was a crew member. I decided it was time to start learning all these rules and at least appear as if I was abiding by them. The band leader, Gary, had warned me when I first took the job. He told me there were a lot of rules. Now I had to learn them. The first rule I had to learn was that I couldn't have any more passengers hanging over the rails of the crew deck at two o'clock in the morning. Got it.

Now, before we get back to the story of what happened to the band in The Cat's Meow (and I promise you are going to like this one), I am going to do the cruise ship a favor in the next few paragraphs and recruit more musicians to work out at sea than anyone has ever recruited before. One of the most amazing aspects of being a musician (especially the drummer) on a cruise ship is that you hardly ever have to move your equipment. I have broken down and set up drum sets so many times that just thinking about it gives me the feeling I would have if I were forced to watch a *Glee* marathon. And I hate *Glee,* for the record. On the cruise ship, all the equipment stays in the theater, or in the club, or in the cigar bar night after night. The guitar amps, lights, drums, cables, and keyboards all stay in the same place for the entire cruise, except for those pesky jazz sets when I sometimes have to move the drum set. As a drummer, all I have to do is bring my drumsticks. All the guitar players have to do is walk in with their guitar, plug in, grab the pick they left on their amp the night before, and play. It's amazing. It's wonderful. It's a dream. It is liberation from a never-ending equipment hauling marathon called gigging on land. I didn't miss it for a second.

I never grew tired of waking up and walking a few hundred feet to The Cat's Meow with my drumsticks in hand, and then sitting down to practice for a few hours before the gig. It was a special time and place for me then. I grooved to whatever my imagination could come up with or worked out rhythms and sections of songs that needed to be smoothed over, and I could do it all in a quiet, empty lounge with the ocean rushing by outside and while the ship sailed through the relentless waves. There is a different rhythm to the ocean and the waves nearly every day. It was extremely enjoyable to get in that room, be alone, and practice my drumming while feeling the motion of the sea. The Cat's Meow was an exceptional rehearsal space. Unfortunately, it didn't last for long.

After the first week on the cruise ship, the band was really cooking. We were packing the club every night. I still loved the free food. At that time, I would have loved any food that was free. The filet mignon limit had not been breached, and I was still excited every time the round, little, molded meat chunks were served. I couldn't believe I was getting paid to play music on a cruise ship with such a great band that was fronted by such an incredible singer. I mean, the girl in this band could sing better than almost anyone I have ever worked with. The fact that she has not yet made a career in the major leagues of the music industry is a testament to how hard it is to make it in this business. You need much more than talent alone. I was even falling for one of the dancers, and I think she was falling for me. The girl was a stunningly beautiful twirly (a slang word for dancers on a cruise ship because they twirl around so much) from New Zealand. I loved the ship life.

Most of all, I immensely enjoyed the complete lack of responsibility and financial freedom. On the ship, I didn't have to worry about much. Many of the tasks and obligations that took up so much of my time on land just didn't exist out on the cruise ship. I was completely not used to having so much free time. It turned out I was right about having time to read books after all. But I didn't read books. Instead, I practiced my drumming for hours on end. This was not much different than my life on land where I was often setting aside around six to ten hours a day to practice my drumming. However, out on the ship I didn't have to put aside other responsibilities in order to have time to practice. Out on the ship, my number one priority could be practicing, performing, and socializing. The hustle was gone. The days of struggling to make ends meet as a musician and a writer were finally put to rest for a while. And at the time, I never wanted it to end.

I spent most of my time on the ship practicing my drumming and rehearsing with the band. No one ever sees all the hours a musician spends practicing. No one ever sees all the hours musicians spend marketing their bands, hustling every day for gigs, making that millionth logo for the new band they are working with, making spreadsheets of venues where they may be able to perform, or designing websites. No one sees the often ridiculous lengths musicians go to in an effort to perfect their sound like attaching a tree branch to the back of a guitar in hopes it will make the tone better. No one ever sees the countless hours spent studying recordings, pouring over endless books of technique and sheet music, and reading interviews with the greatest drummers of all time to get a snippet of wisdom that can be applied to your own playing or performance.

No one ever sees the thousands and thousands of dollars spent on musical equipment either; every musician knows that musical equipment is the most overpriced merchandise ever sold. I mean, who decided that spindly drumsticks should cost ten dollars? And the person who decided that most drummers can afford to pay $450 for a ride cymbal is severely detached from reality. I spent several nights eating tomato soup for dinner and junior mints for desert because of people like that. No one ever sees the hours spent tuning, polishing, repairing, moving, moving, and moving the equipment. People only see what they want to see, and all they want to see is the end result—the performance. So most people come to a performance, they sit down, and have a few drinks at The Cat's Meow or whatever hole-in-the wall you're playing at. They get up and dance for a bit, and then they walk out of the performance feeling great and think, *Man, those musicians have it so easy. All they have to do is work for three friggin' hours a day on this cruise ship and that's it. All they have to do is play music—do something they love for a living. It must be nice.*

It is nice. It is incredible to do what you love for a living. It is wonderful to wake up excited every day about how you're going to earn your keep. And it is truly outstanding to be able to do it on a ship that is sailing around the world and stopping at the most beautiful beaches, islands, and cities on the planet. However, the biggest lie ever told is that a musician only works three hours a day. And let me tell you, this myth is believed with absolute certainty by the other crew members on a cruise ship just as much as it is believed by people on land. Sometimes, the other crew members downright hate us for it; and sometimes crew members will let you know just how much they dislike it to your face with all the expectations that you're just going to shake your head, agree with them, laugh, and say, "*Yeah, I'm a lazy musician.*" But let me clear it up once and for all. Musicians (at least the successful ones) are some of the hardest working, most persevering, most driven, and motivated people you will ever meet.

Musicians have to be like this if they want to be successful. There is luck, but that only happens for a few. The rest of us have to work extremely hard to get anywhere in music. Behind every good musician is enough chewed up drumsticks, broken guitar strings, bloody fingers, and torn off calluses to fill a stadium. Musicians must have the perseverance of Winston Churchill and the work ethic of Nicholas Cage. Put this together with the talent of Mickey Mantle and you got yourself a star, or a musician who is barely making it, or the world's greatest bass player on the street with a tip jar playing the most moving rendition of *America the Beautiful* you have ever heard. If you're not a musician, you may not have gotten that joke, so let me point it.

They are all the same thing.

They say it takes 10,000 hours of practice to master an instrument. I don't even know what that means. What does mastering an instrument even mean? However, I would say it takes 10,000 hours of practice just to get a gig these days. Most musicians I know, including myself, have spent way more than 10,000 hours playing our instruments. The audience sees the three hours on stage. Musicians live the other 9,997 hours in the woodshed, in the practice room, in the studio, humming tunes in their heads, and going over ideas. Many musicians sit in the same chair for every single one of those 9,997 hours, and the chair rests on a mountain of wood chips, calluses, and brilliant ideas. Believe it. It's true.

By the second week onboard, I was finally able to step off the ship for the first time. I was hoping to step off the ship onto an island and straight onto a beautiful beach that just happened to be hosting the annual Hooters wet T-shirt contest or something. However, I wasn't able to just walk down the gangway and step right into the bosom of the beach so to speak. Instead, I was introduced to the cruel and unfortunate practice of tendering.

I had to wait in line, swipe my crew member identification card, walk down the gangway, and climb aboard yet another boat. It felt extremely counterproductive. I wanted to get off the ship, but instead I got off the ship and then got on a boat. Maybe after the boat they would put me on a raft, and then in those arm floats that children wear, and then make me hold a life preserver as they pulled me to shore. And it was all a bit frightening as well. I mean, if the ship didn't want to go to this particular port, then why the hell would I? Were there pirates in these waters or something? Why would I want to go out there on a little stupid looking orange boat? I walked down the gangway anyhow and didn't see a single sandy shore for at least a mile. There was no concrete pier that led to a fake village like you usually find at the ports. There was only the surrounding sea and an orange colored boat bobbing up and down at the end of the rickety gangway. If you've never experienced tendering than you're definitely better off than the rest of us. I've seen some truly nightmarish events transpire as a result of tendering.

If you're not familiar, tenders are the boats that take passengers to shore when the waters surrounding a destination are too shallow for the cruise ship to sail. Sometimes passengers also have to tender because there is no dock at the port, or the port is already at full capacity. The cruise ship will anchor offshore (yes, the cruise ship does have an anchor and yes, it is unbelievably massive). And then the passengers have to ride in these little boats called tenders to shore. These boats can carry about 50 passengers at a time, and you are *always* taking a risk when you get into a tender. The tender isn't likely to sink or anything. It's just that you are putting yourself at the mercy of the sea.

Most people cruise in the Caribbean, and the weather there is extremely volatile. It can change in an instant. The best example I can offer (or possibly the worst in this case) occurred while we were anchored off the coast of Saint Thomas. The seas were building, but the weather didn't seem as if it was something to be concerned about. Then suddenly, a swirl of dark storm clouds swept over the ship faster than a crew member can eat a bowl of rice. The waves quickly built to a choppy, churning, agitated mess. At this exact time, a fleet of maybe six or seven tenders were trying to return to the ship. The tender boats began to violently bob up and down. They would disappear behind every wave. Everyone aboard the cruise ship gathered on the edge of the lido deck and watched the helpless tender passengers that had become marooned in the grips of a savage Caribbean Sea.

Every time the tender disappeared behind a wave, the cruise ship passengers would gasp. Everyone feared that the tenders were going to overturn at any minute. They feared the Coast Guard would have to be called to the scene of a horrible tender disaster, and when they arrived the only thing they could do was dredge the bottom of the Caribbean Sea and recover the absurdly sunburned bodies of white people with strangely braided and beaded hair who were clutching soggy boxes of Tortuga Rum Cakes, perfectly sealed bags of illicit Cuban cigars, unopened bottles of rum, their winnings from hermit crab races, and other miscellaneous shit that passengers buy in the Caribbean.

The worst part of the whole ordeal was that the tenders couldn't rope up to the side of the ship. They couldn't return to the port they had just left. The seas were just too high. They were in no man's land; forsaken castaways on a cruise from hell. All they could do was just bob around out there in the storm. Soon, the hundreds of tender passengers were puking over the side and hanging on for their dear lives. This went on for hours and hours. The passengers back on the cruise ship could do nothing but watch the whole wretched disaster unfold before their eyes. All they could do was sit on the lido deck and eat greasy chicken fingers and pizza and sip their frozen margaritas while they watched those poor souls turn as green as avocados. Eventually, the seas died down and the tender passengers, wobbling and dehydrated and ready to punch the lights out of the captain, stumbled back aboard the ship. When you step onto a tender you are putting yourself at the mercy of the sea. Do it at your own risk, and bring a paper bag, Dramamine, one of those goofy sea sickness patches, a year's supply of sea-sickness bracelets, and plenty of water with you. You never know just how long you might be on that thing.

To get to my first island that I would visit on a cruise ship, I had to take a tender. Luckily, the seas were calm. The Caribbean water was so blue and so beautiful that the singer in the band made the observation that the water looked like Blue Kool-Aid. The water was beautiful. I got off the ship and walked up and down the beach with a few of my musician friends in the show band and the New Zealand dancer I was working on. The cruise ship was anchored just off the coast of the island. The ship's reggae band was performing under a tiki hut. A few crew members were grilling hamburgers and hot dogs. The island had been transformed into an idyllic beach party. This is something I will never forget. This was the exact moment that I absolutely, completely, and entirely fell in love with ship life. I was hooked. There was no turning back now. I knew this was what I wanted to do for a very long time. I knew I wanted to be a cruise ship crew member for as long as I possibly could.

Everything was going perfectly. The band just kept getting better. The practicing was paying off, and we were packing the club more and more every night. We were selling lots of drinks like we were supposed to, because everyone knows a musician's job at a bar gig is not to entertain people, it's to sell drinks. The ship followed its itinerary to a tee. We made our stops at Nassau and Half Moon Cay. The ship roped up at Grand Cayman where I couldn't get off because I had more corporate videos to watch. Each video was worse than the last. They were apparently made for people who couldn't understand English very well. The same ideas were reiterated over and over again. It was like listening to an Adele album. OK. We get it. You're sad.

It was the last night of my second cruise. The band had one more song to perform to finish up our second-to-last set in The Cat's Meow. Star Man had an idea for the last song of our set. He put down his bass. Star Man was basically running the show. Gary was the band leader, the real brains and talent behind the operation, but Star Man had that controlling personality that wouldn't be denied no matter how hard the rest of the band tried. The situation was basically like this—let Star Man run the show and let him be the center of attention. Otherwise, he would sabotage the whole performance. If we didn't let him have his way, he would complain so much that we would just give up, mainly because we couldn't bear to listen to him complain any longer. So, everyone just went with it and let Star Man run the band. He picked the songs for the most part. He decided who was soloing and when, regulated the tempo of the songs, controlled how bright the lights were on stage, and who they were shining on, which was mostly him. He was a real band Nazi. However, in all honesty, I have to admit that he did an absolutely dynamite job. He knew how to run a show. He knew when to showboat during a song, when to slow it down for a slow dance, and when to dim the lights. He was a natural. He had that perfect combination of showmanship and crowd intuition that can really light up the stage. It was sensational.

So, Star Man had this great idea. He told everyone in the band to come out to the front of the stage. He turned off all the guitar amps, and then he walked over to the sound board and killed the switch. The microphones went dead. All the hums and buzzes coming from the sound board, amps, and keyboards were killed. The stage went completely silent. He dimmed the lights and had all of us in the band sit on the edge of the stage. The audience was captivated. There wasn't a sound in the room but the chinking of ice cubes against glasses and a few people at the bar whispering to the bartender.

We sat at the edge of the stage. Star Man asked us to put our arms on each other's shoulders, and then he grabbed his bass and started plucking a few notes. The crowd was deadly quiet as Star Man played the first five notes of the song. The band was all embraced on the front of the stage, and in an instant we knew what we were about to do. Star Man had plucked out the first five notes of one of the most recognizable songs ever written— "Lean on Me" by Bill Withers. Shelia, the sexy-hot female singer of the group, took the lead. Her voice was more pure, clean, and perfectly pitched than any singer I have ever heard. She had the power of Aretha Franklin combined with the crisp, flawless, and steady qualities of Alison Krauss.

It was magical. And the crowd that was packed into The Cat's Meow was absolutely moved, even though they were packed into the club among the cat food bag paintings and the booths shaped like cans of cat food. The audience was captivated. The rest of the band joined in for the moving *a cappella* version of the chorus.

It was perfect. It was the best ending to a set I have ever done in a club as tacky as The Cat's Meow. However, there was more to the moment than what we were singing. We had come together as a band, yes, but there was more than that. It felt as if the moment would hold more meaning than what had just occurred on the surface. It felt like more than simple showmanship or a unification of friends and musicians. There was some finality to it all. There was something in the air that made the poignancy of the moment magnified and electrified. It was enough to give you goose bumps and send chills down your spine. It was touching, but it somehow felt like the end to more than just the set. It felt like the closing of a long chapter, the ending to a long struggle, and the victory speech at the end of a battle all wrapped up into one moment.

When we walked off the stage, I noticed that the cruise director had been there watching us. He called Gary over to his table, and I assumed the cruise director would talk to him about that fine musical moment he had just witnessed. Instead, Gary turned around with an absolute look of disgust on his face. The entire band knew something was wrong. Gary called us over to the side of the stage and gathered us in a circle. He took a deep breath.

"The cruise director just fired us," Gary said.

I was shocked. Shelia, the singer, immediately started to cry. Gary continued.

"He just fired us because of what happened the night before Josh got here."

I was stunned. Everything had been going so well. The band was rocking. I was making friends with dancers. This was no time to leave the ship. This was no time to get fired.

"I don't know what I'm going to do," Shelia said through tears and a curled lip. "What am I going to do? I have a baby at home. I don't know what I'm going to do. How can they just fire us like this? Without any warning? Is this our last night?"

"It gets better," Gary said. "The cruise director wants us to finish up the show. He wants us to play our last set. And then he said we have to start packing our equipment. We have to be off the ship right when we get to port at 6 a.m. We are the first ones off. They're not giving us a ticket home or any gas money or anything like that. They're just kicking us to the curb, and they want us to play our last set."

"So, why are we getting fired?" I asked. Apparently, everyone else in the band already knew. This was the first time I had heard of the band's sordid past.

"The night before you got here," Gary explained, "we were partying pretty hard. We were all really excited that you were going to be coming and joining us and we got a little carried away. We ended up drinking a little too much and showed up to the gig a little drunk, which is against the rules."

This was a first. The cruise ship gig, with the exception of performing in the church band, is probably one of the only gigs on the planet where you are prohibited from drinking alcohol. But the rules are the rules, and Gary knew it. That's what Gary had said to me when he hired me. He said, "As long as you follow the rules, you're going to be all right." But this was ridiculous. The whole band was getting canned because a few guys showed up to the gig drunk. It was bizarre. Yet, it spoke volumes about how serious the cruise ship companies take the rules. It was absurd, but there was nothing we could do about it. At least that's what we thought. Shelia, on the other hand, had a completely different opinion on the matter.

While Gary was explaining why we were getting

fired, the scorned wheels inside Shelia's mind started to turn. I always knew she had spunk. This one had a little bit of fire in her. She wasn't going down without a fight. Before we knew it, she had turned the sound board back on and had the microphone in her hand. The crowd was still packed and ready for our last set— a last set that everyone in the band knew wasn't going to happen. There was no way that any of us were about to play a last set for the company that just fired us.

There were tears rolling down Shelia's cheeks. Everyone in the crowd was on the edge of their seats. They knew something very entertaining was about to happen. Shelia was a beautiful 24-year-old black woman who represented the very definition of a singing diva, and she was standing on the stage and crying in the spotlight while wearing strappy, knee-high heels and a sparkling sequined dress that left no curves whatsoever to the imagination. And let me tell you, Shelia had more curves than the price graph for Enron stock. Everyone knew something very entertaining was about to happen. Call it a gut feeling. Shelia looked right into the crowd. Through her sobs and tears, she said something like this.

"Ladies and gentlemen, I want to thank you for listening to us during your cruise, but I am here to let you know that we will not be playing our last set tonight, because the cruise company has fired us." There were gasps in the crowd. Many of the passengers in the crowd had gotten to know us very well during their cruise. It felt like the band had made a bunch of new friends. These passengers loved the music we were playing, and some of them came to listen to us every night. They were definitely on our side. I watched as a few of the passengers stood up and walked straight over to the cruise director. At the same time, the cruise director was attempting to dodge the concerned passengers and trying to desperately fight his way towards the stage. He had some sort of delusional fantasy that maybe he would be able calm Shelia down and convince her to put the microphone away. He wanted to end the episode of hysteria as quickly as possible. The crowd was demanding answers. Shelia just kept going. She kept feeding the fire.

"We are better than this. We didn't do nothin' wrong. This company is going to fire us, kick us to the curb like a bunch of bums, and leave us without a ticket home. I have worked too hard for this kind of treatment. I have a baby at home. I can't lose this job. We didn't do anything wrong. They are just going to fire us for nothing, and make us get off the ship right when we get into port."

The tears were really flowing now. Many of the passengers were starting to get very upset. They were on our side. And when they saw Shelia up on stage crying and yelling about the absolute injustice of the situation, they just wouldn't stand for it. The cruise director was practically mobbed with a crowd of people asking for an explanation. He made an admirable, yet nonetheless ineffective, effort at diplomacy. He put his hands out toward the crowd to stop them from crowding him.

"This is a private matter between the company and the band. Absolutely nothing wrong has happened here."

The crowd wasn't buying his unconvincing and amateurish Jedi mind tricks. To make matters worse, one of the production shows had just ended. A crowd of people were leaving the theater and flooding onto the promenade. They all had to walk directly past The Cat's Meow which was absolutely riotous. The crowd was drawn to the commotion and the sound of Shelia's sobbing and angry voice like, well, cats to giant paintings of cat food bags. The scene in the club quickly devolved into something resembling a middle school fight where the surrounding crowd starts to cheer on the students who are swinging fists and pulling weaves out of each other's heads. Passengers poured into the club. They demanded justice for the curvaceous black woman in the sequined dress and strappy high heels that they saw crying up on stage in the spotlight. I wish I had a picture of the moment. It was as close as I had ever been to a protest besides the time I participated in a walk-out in elementary school to revolt against the removal of country-fried steak from the cafeteria menu. I was as mad that night in The Cat's Meow as I was back then in elementary school. And that's saying a lot. I love country-fried steak.

The crowd grew so large that it poured out into the promenade. The cruise director eventually fought his way to the sound board and shut it off. However, his efforts were futile. Powering down the sound board did little to quiet Shelia. She was a singer with a powerful voice. She had vocal chords that could shatter crystal glasses, and she was mad. She kept ranting and raving. No one in the band tried to calm her down. We thought she did have a point, and it was nice to have a scorned woman on my side for a change. Eventually, the cruise director told Shelia that he had called security, and so Shelia dramatically stormed out of The Cat's Meow in a rage. A whirlwind of applause followed her down the promenade deck.

The crowd quickly died down. Just minutes earlier the club was filled with loyal supporters involved in a protest against injustice and tragedy. Once Shelia was gone, the crowd simply shrank and faded away. Eventually, the only people left in The Cat's Meow were Gary, Star Man, and me. We solemnly packed up our gear and rolled up chords in an empty room with cat food bags on the wall and a fake tire for a dance floor. Star Man didn't stick around long. He left shortly after Shelia stormed out of the club. I assumed he was going to fill up his milk jugs one last time. I kept packing up my drum gear. Rumor has it that Star Man was urinating on the staff captain's door just about the time I was packing away my last cymbal. Star Man had his own way of protesting, I guess.

At six in the morning, we were carrying our gear off the ship. We had no idea what to do next or what to say to each other about what had happened. Gary apologized that things had turned out the way they had. I was very disappointed about the situation, but I decided to keep that to myself. Shelia was still playing the victim and complaining about the unfairness of life to whoever would listen to her. Everyone sincerely felt sorry for her. However, on a ship the only person that can change anything is the captain, and the band had been fired directly through captain's orders. Any dream of a reversal of the captain's decision was a fantasy at this point.

I had one last chance to go aboard the ship to grab a few of my duffel bags filled with books and the last of my gear. I walked into my crew cabin and saw the show band drummer sleeping in the tiny bottom bunk. He was drooling on his pillow. I had an idea. I grabbed a notepad and wrote a letter to the show band's music director. The letter asked if I could audition for the orchestra. I wrote down my email address and phone number. It was a shot in the dark, but I refused to just walk away from the job without trying for a second chance. The cruise ship gig was too good and way too much fun. I climbed a flight of stairs to the music director's room. He answered the door half asleep. It was six a.m. after all. The music director looked thoroughly unimpressed that I had knocked on his door that early in the morning, but he took my letter anyway.

"I'll see what I can do," is all he said before he shut the door.

Down in the parking lot of the port, the band loaded the rest of the equipment into the band van. It was a sad procession that we all knew was going to end with every one of us having to rejoin real life. The hustle was back. It had been waiting for us. It helped itself and all of its suitcases into the band van. The hustle was definitely back.

A few of the friends I had made, incluc Zealand dancer, came down to the port to s I stood at the edge of the port, looking completely frazzled and sapped from a complete lack of sleep and the shock of the previous seven hours. The ship blew its horn. The sound shook through my entire body. It was the final note to the band's final set, and a shockingly loud end to my two-week long career as a cruise ship musician. The ropes were untied from the dock. The ship slowly sailed away without us. It was on its way back to a place where the water looks like blue Kool-Aid, back to that island of paradise where the reggae band is playing under a tiki hut and the crew is grilling hot dogs, hamburgers, and iguana or something. The cruise ship was sailing back to the Caribbean. It was sailing away without us. It felt as if the band wasn't even good enough for The Cat's Meow, the tackiest, gaudiest, and most unfit performance space on the planet. The band members said goodbye to one another. I loaded my duffel bags full of books back into my car. I turned around and looked at the ship one last time. The ship was drifting away. It left a long foamy trail in its wake. From this perspective, my life on the cruise ship felt like nothing but a fantasy. It felt like nothing more than a dream. Somehow though, I knew deep in my heart that this wasn't going to be the last time that I would work as a cruise ship crew member. And boy was I right. Somehow, I also knew that next time I wasn't going to bring so many damn books.

6

WHY ARE ALL THE OFFICERS ITALIAN?

For crew members, the quality of ship life is largely defined by the character of the captain and his officers. In fact, much more than you probably think seems to depend on the attitude and management style of the elite ranks on a cruise ship, from the morale of a ship's crew and the collective character of a ship's environment to the safety and wellbeing of the crew and passengers aboard a cruise ship. Crew members want to find themselves assigned to ships led by an effective captain with exceptional leadership skills, outstanding experience, and a positive attitude. They also want a captain and officers that are respectful to crew members, concerned about the morale of the crew, and most importantly, dedicated to the safety of everyone on board. Sometimes, the stars actually align just right and crew members are assigned to ships like this.

However, these ships are few and far between. They are anomalies. I have been lucky enough to get assigned to several ships with phenomenal captains and officers. Of all the ships I have ever been assigned, these ships were the most efficient, safe, and fun. When the crew is happy and morale is running high, the crew takes more pride in their work. They value their job and want to do everything they can to keep it. The crew works harder. The ship is cleaner. Fresh coats of paint are more prevalent. The engine mechanics, safety officers, and inspectors are working harder and making the ship safer for everyone. It all seems to trickle down from the captain—his attitude, work ethic, and his leisure ethic, as well. Nine times out of ten, the captain can make the difference between a ship with a miserable crew that runs aground on a rocky Italian coast, and a safe ship with a hardworking and happy crew that all make it home alive. Nine times out of ten, this captain and his officers are Italian.

Most people who go on a cruise will likely notice the lack of ethnic diversity among cruise ship officers and captains. However, most cruisers may not realize that the overwhelming majority of the cooks and security guards on cruise ships are Indian, most of the cabin stewards and crew members that work in the laundry and housekeeping departments are Filipino, almost all of the entertainment department and cruise directors are Westerners, and most of the casino employees are from Russia, Romania, or Ukraine.

What most people don't know is that the ship is a highly stratified environment where the imaginary boundaries between departments are like borders dividing countries that are usually oceans apart. Walking onto a ship is like stepping back in time. It is like stepping onto a floating city where people from all countries are welcome and come to experience the promised golden opportunities of a life out at sea, but where it is quickly realized that your country of origin almost certainly defines your place and mobility within the ship society. It is like a modern-day floating caste system in a lot of ways. And the caste system is not enforced or regulated by a single government, business, or religious institution. It is created, molded, reinforced, and upheld by the invisible hand of the global economy. It is immensely interesting.

There are many ways to look at the issues of stratification, wages, and mobility on a cruise ship. To get an idea of how these departments become so ethnically unvaried, it is important that we start at the beginning. We must start by examining how people really get jobs on cruise ships in India, Russia, Indonesia, or America. Most of the people that are working on cruise ships are from what we in the West would consider lesser developed countries. They come from countries where the prospect of getting paid $300 a week is a prospect worth pursuing wholeheartedly. And the cruise ship companies are more than happy to put them to work for more than twelve hours a day, six-and-a-half days a week for that $300 paycheck. Believe it. It's true.

Apart from coming from lesser developed countries, many crew members also come from countries that are currently struggling economically. I would not be surprised if the number of Americans working on cruise ships began to dramatically increase beginning in 2008 and continued to grow as the Great Recession deepened. When I first joined the ships in 2006, there were considerably more Russians on board; then the oil boom started in that country, and the number of Eastern and Central Europeans noticeably, swiftly dwindled. It is amazing to see how a country's poor economy can impact individuals.

I remember talking to my first cabin steward about his life and why he was working on ships. I just wanted to get to know him, hear his story, and learn about his country and culture. Everyone has an interesting story if you just lend your ear for a few minutes, practice being a good listener, and ask the right questions. My cabin steward didn't let me down.

It turns out he had been a doctor in Indonesia. He lived and worked in Bali. This crew member, a kind-hearted, hard-working, and patient young man of maybe 30, had gone to medical school. He had graduated near the top of his class, went to work at a hospital, and began working his way up the ranks. He was working hard to get a good job as a doctor when his life came crashing down around him. The story that he told to me was one of the greatest illustrations of how cruel life can be. Here was a doctor and, as a result of circumstances completely out of his control, he was making my bed, cleaning my toilet, and cleaning thirty other crew toilets as well.

He had worked and lived in Bali in the resort district of Kuta. He was raising a family there. On October 12, 2002, a man walked into Paddy's Pub, a popular bar in the tourist district of Kuta. Strapped to his back was a backpack filled with blocks of C4 plastic explosives. He walked somewhere near the middle of the packed club and detonated the C4. Those who survived the explosion poured out into the street. There was a white Mitsubishi van parked in front of the club where the survivors were gathering. The van was parked just across the street from Paddy's Pub in front of the neighboring Sari nightclub. This van was also packed with C4 explosives.

Just as the survivors poured into the streets from the attack at Paddy's Pub, the bomb inside the Mitsubishi van was detonated by a suicide bomber. The attack was funded by Al Qaeda, and it remains the deadliest terrorist attack in Indonesia. The violent blast killed 202 people, most of them Australian, Indonesian, British, and American tourists. The attack devastated the local economy. It devastated the tourism industry which was the main source of income for many of the people who lived in the country. Work dried up, and as a result, the doctor who was now my cabin steward came to work on the cruise ships. He came to work scrubbing toilets, cleaning showers, and making beds for $300 a week.

While this is an exceptional story, many people end up working on cruise ships because their local economy went down the tube. They are motivated by the desire to escape a lack of opportunity in their home country. And this is the same whether a crew member is coming from Indonesia, Russia, or the United States. There are those crew members who have the luxury of working on a cruise ship simply because they want the adventure, travel, and to lead a life exploring sandy beaches and sunny islands. However, this is an exception, and not the rule.

All around the world, in the developed countries as well as in the less developed countries, there are recruiters, agents, and cruise ship company offices set up to find these people, get them hired, and ship them out for a life at sea. The interesting thing is that in each country, there seems to be a singular focus on recruiting people to work in particular jobs on the cruise ship. In India, they must have offices that only recruit cooks and security guards, while in Indonesia, if you want to work on the ship you will go to a recruitment office and find that housekeeping jobs are the only jobs that ever happen to be available. The dancers, musicians, cruise directors, social hosts, and singers are mostly hired from America, England, and Australia. And it seems that the cruise ship companies prefer to recruit their captains and officers from that big *stivale* (boot) in the Mediterranean called Italy.

So, when crew members first step aboard a cruise ship and walk down the I-95, they step into a distinctly culturally-diverse environment. They are walking among people from all around the world and can hear almost every language on the planet being spoken. Then a crew member will walk to their first department meeting and find that nearly everyone there is from the same ethnic background, except one crew member from Canada with dreadlocks who thought it would be a good idea to work as a pastry chef. The crew member is shocked to see that nearly everyone at the meeting is from the same country.

Of course, there are exceptions. You will find Russians on the dance cast and in the orchestra. Sure, there are Canadian cooks, American waiters, and Filipino singers, but not many. I have seen only a few westerners get recruited somehow into cook positions and security guard jobs, but most of them last no longer than a month. Fortunately, the entertainment department may have the most diverse department on the ship. This can make it a very interesting place to work.

However, on many cruise ships the absolute least culturally diverse department on the ship is found on the Bridge. When you visit the Bridge on a cruise ship, you definitely will be hard pressed to find someone who does not have dark, slicked-back hair. The probability is extremely high that everyone working there will be drinking a cappuccino, and it would be a rare occasion if anyone welcomed you with a greeting other than "Ciao." It's just not going to happen. Almost everyone working on the bridge is Italian. Yet, you can walk into the orchestra pit and find a Canadian trombone player, an American drummer, a Russian keyboard player, a South American bass player, an English trumpet player, and a French sax player. People come from all over the world to play in the cruise ship orchestra.

Because of the cultural division between departments on a cruise ship, there is plenty of grumbling and dissatisfaction about the remarkable disparity in wages between crew members from different countries and therefore between people in different departments. A lot of the time, the complaints are extremely valid. However, larger and louder than the chorus of wage disparity critics are a very vocal and majority group of crew members who are absolutely content and downright happy to make the kind of money they earn on the cruise ships.

Sure, the cruise companies can afford to pay many of these workers more money. Sure, dancers and musicians and cabin stewards alike deserve more than what they are being paid, but no one is holding a gun to our heads and making us work for what they are paying us. For the most part, all of the crew members actively sought their respective jobs on the cruise ship. They knew what they were getting into (for the most part), and not only were they happy to accept the job, but they were willing (maybe not as happy as they were on their first contract, but willing nonetheless) to take the job again, and again, and again, sometimes for the rest of their lives.

The reason for this is simple, as well. The cruise companies are paying these crew members far better than what the crew member can earn back home. The cruise ship is providing crew members with more adventure, more travel, and sometimes (and this is probably a very small minority) unthinkably better food than they can get in their home country. The cruise ship is a better opportunity, and if crew members find a better situation back home, then they stay at home and work there and never go out on the cruise ship again. At least not until we get the tropical island blues and find ourselves dreaming of eating heaping plates of free filet mignon in the shade of palm fronds on an island in the Caribbean somewhere. Then we pick up the phone, call our cruise ship agent, and pathetically beg for another contract.

So, back to the initial question, it seems that the reason all officers are Italian is really a result of the recruitment process. This recruitment process may also explain the lack of ethnic diversity within most of the departments on a cruise ship. However, maybe the cruise ships are this way simply because it works better. Maybe time has taught a valuable lesson to individual cruise ship departments that they just simply run more smoothly when there is a majority of people within that department who are coming from the same culture, the same background, and the same understanding of each other.

I can say first hand that working with people from all over the world (and working on a cruise ship you definitely get the chance to work with people from just about every country on the planet) can be extremely interesting, fascinating, incomparably eye opening, and life changing, not to mention lots of fun and a real adventure. It can also be very difficult and frustrating. A great example and illustration of this fact can be experienced every day around eleven a.m. This is when lunch is served in the crew mess, and it can be a madhouse, especially when there are chicken tenders on the menu.

You know you're living a life that is exceptionally deprived of decent food when chicken fingers and the gooey, orange-colored, honey-mustard syrup send you and your fellow crew members into a frenzy to match the best water chumming scenes during Discovery Channel's *Shark Week*. This is exactly what it is like. Not just when chicken fingers are served, but every day of the week. And the differences between cultures can cause the situation to devolve into absolute chaos.

You see, there are some places in the world where lines do not exist. It seems that an orderly process for each individual to proceed through a line to receive food, board a bus, get off the ship, or get a drink at the bar is an abstract and ridiculous concept to many people in many parts of the world. In these situations, madness replaces a simple and orderly line. On chicken day in the crew mess, it is every man for himself— people shoving and crowding up against the protective plastic sneeze guards at the buffet island. Chaos also ensues when there is a bus available to take crew members into town. Mobs of crew members create a hectic bottleneck at the small bus door. The same disorganized confusion can be found at the gangway when there is a port day after several consecutive days at sea. Crew members will crowd the gangway without any regard for order or civility. No one person or approach is necessarily "right" in these situations. The different approaches are simply cultural differences. Nonetheless, the differences that do exist often make the situation extremely difficult to handle.

Maybe there is an understanding within the recruiting offices for cruise ships that these cultural differences can often manifest themselves into stressful situations for crew members. Maybe it has been proven that the departments on a cruise ship run more smoothly when everyone within the department is able to cope without lines and the order and civility that they create. Maybe the navigation duties run more efficiently and safely when everyone on the bridge can speak Italian without having to resort to broken English that is absolutely incomprehensible to any English-speaking person.

Maybe things run more efficiently when everyone understands each other's humor, slang, and body language. Maybe it is more enjoyable for crew members who are Filipino to work in a dominantly Filipino housekeeping department where the majority wholeheartedly believe that karaoke and all-male dance groups are really cool; or a casino staff dominated by Eastern Europeans who all still think chain smoking, 1990's rave music, and putting sour cream in your soup is hip; or a mostly western entertainment department where everyone can get together and complain about how much they miss the Cheesecake Factory, and everyone knows what the hell they're talking about. Yet, when all is said and done, all crew members from every department still get together to socialize in the crew bar, or out on the open deck where we tell jokes that only half the crew members there actually understand. More importantly, we are offered the opportunity to understand what it is really like to live and come from another country that is so different from our own.

An interesting thing is that the cruise ships' ethnically unvaried departments and the origin based stratification will probably always exist in the cruise industry. As long as cruise ships are bobbing around out in all those oceans all around the world, cruise ship departments will be there subtlety defining and clearly reflecting the current state of the global economy. And just as the economic conditions of countries are constantly changing, so will the origins of the people that occupy the different departments on a cruise ship.

A fascinating perspective is that a cruise ship is like a microcosm that reflects the world around it. Yet, it is at once both a macroscopic view of the world (the global economy and the different economic conditions of the people that occupy it) and also a place where one can get a microscopic view of these cultures through the crew members who are all condensed together onto this sailing city—a sailing city that at its heart flies every flag of every nation, and does so amazingly peacefully. If you want to find out how we can achieve peace in this world, just go on a cruise and observe the crew members. You'll discover pretty quickly that the way to create a peaceful planet is to give a man a job with adequate pay, an endless supply of food and water, a tolerable amount of living space, a government that is respected and properly functioning, and a place to watch the World Cup. Do all this and you pretty much have peace on earth. A cruise ship is a beautiful thing if you just look at it with the right perspective.

So, while most of the officers on cruise ships are Italian (and while almost no crew member-ah can ever-ah completely understand-ah what they are saying-ah), the cruise ship's lack of cultural diversity within departments somehow, for me at least, felt natural and agreeable. This division of culture felt as if it enabled crew members to retain some sense of borders and cultural individualism in an environment that was so dominated by cultural diversity.

Yet, at the end of a cruise ship contract, no matter what country a crew member comes from, each crew member will have shared an experience that will define them nearly as much as their nationality. This is because after crew members spend six months on a ship together, it no longer matters if you're an officer from Italy, an Indonesian cabin steward from Bali, or an American drummer from Florida. When each crew member walks down that gangway, they will discover that they will be forever connected to, united with, and understood by every crew member that has ever walked down that gangway before them or after. This is the common bond of being a cruise ship crew member. An amazing transformation occurs on a cruise ship. A crew member walks onto a ship, and they do not understand the language and the culture of the other crew members around them. During their contracts, they experience that powerful force that unites people when they go through something incredibly unique and life changing such as working on a cruise ship. And when these same crew members leave the ship, they discover that the only people in the world who will ever be able to fully understand them are other crew members. These crew members realize that they will only be completely understood by the same people that they once absolutely did not understand at all.

7

OK. WHAT IS IT LIKE TO WORK AS A MUSICIAN IN THE ORCHESTRA ON A CRUISE SHIP?

No amount of rehearsing could have prepared me for the audition I was about to have. I had blown all my cash in the Caribbean. The firing was completely unexpected, and now I was back on the hustle train trying to put together as many leads for jobs as possible. I was surprised when I got a call back from Disney. I had heard some pretty good things about Disney Tokyo while I was out on the ship those two weeks, and so I decided to look them up. It turned out they were having auditions in Orlando, and I got a call back that put me on the audition list.

The agents at Disney Tokyo told me they were looking for a couple of drummers for a comedy routine. The show was heavily choreographed and featured two drummers who were dressed up as chefs. The drummers were expected to play merengue and mambo rhythms on pots and pans using spatulas, spoons, and knives. It wasn't really my kind of gig, but the pay and experience were tops— $4,000 a month and your own studio apartment in Tokyo with a kitchen. There wouldn't be any free filet mignon or probably the caliber of milk that you can find on the cruise ship, but I would have my freedom and a kitchen to cook whatever I wanted, a top paying job, and my own apartment in one of the most expensive and exciting cities in the world. Plus, Disney has an incredible jazz big-band in Tokyo. I thought maybe if I wore the chef's hat for a few months, I might be able to transition to a club or jazz gig, and then possibly progress to the drum chair in the big band and have the splendid opportunity to play Count Basie and Gordon Goodwin charts for a living. That didn't sound bad at all, and besides, by that time I would have saved up like ten grand, so I decided to go for it. I mean, come on, I was going to be laughing all the way to the bank while getting paid four grand a month for beating on pots and pans with spatulas and spoons. It sounded hilarious, so I was in.

I asked the agent, who was Japanese, what the rehearsal would be like. He said I would be playing Latin rhythms on timbales, those big metal drums with thin plastic heads that you hear a lot in Latin and reggae music. I figured I should read up on some traditional approaches to playing timbales. I spent the next two weeks basically living inside a set of timbales drums. I was informed that I would be reading charts for the audition, so I brushed up on reading charts and rhythms for that type of music. I wanted to make it to Tokyo. I wanted the gig, and I definitely wanted to leave the hustle behind again.

There were about thirty other drummers at the audition that was being held at a rehearsal facility for Disney in Orlando, Florida. Judging by the massive-sized drumsticks that most of the other drummers were holding, it was obvious that the majority of drummers were from a marching band background. I didn't know the first thing about marching band drumming, but I knew most of those guys had serious skills in rudiments, technique, and flashy drumstick tricks. One of the Japanese agents walked up to the group of drummers and gave us instructions for the audition in broken English.

"You will be called into audition one at time. After finish you audition, you cannot tell other drummer what it like. If you do, you be eliminated. *Ganbatte kudasai!* (good luck)."

The first drummer was called. He walked down a long hallway and into a room. Two minutes later he came back with a confused look on his face.

"That was interesting," was all he said.

I was one of the last drummers to get called into the audition room. I walked down the hallway and through some heavy double doors. In the room there were three folding tables that formed one long and rather intimidating table where about ten Japanese judges were sitting and smiling. I wasn't sure whether to bow or say "Hello" or what. The judges all just kind of waved awkwardly and motioned towards a single battered trashcan in the center of the room. *What the hell is this?* I thought. *A trash can? Really? The agent said I was going to be playing timbales. I learn timbales, and they give me an audition on a trash can?*

I thought for sure this was some kind of cruel joke. I realized it was very real when one of the judges pointed to the trash can.

"You play trash can," he said. He even managed to say it with a sincere smile. Latin music began playing from speakers mounted in the ceiling. The main Japanese judge pointed to the trash can again.

"With much enthusiasm. Play with much smile on face."

I rocked that trash can like I was in a carnival street parade in Rio and received a nice round of applause from the judges. All those years of practice, tuning, perfecting subtle rolls, and polishing difficult drum patterns had all come down to an ear-splitting audition on a trash can. Unbelievable.

All the other drummers were eventually cut. The audition came down to me and one other guy. The Japanese judges lead both of us back into the audition room where a bubbly Japanese woman taught us a dance routine that we had to memorize and repeat. I knew then and there I wasn't going to get the job. I've got rhythm, but I had never memorized a dance routine in my life. They still sized us both up for uniforms, but I didn't expect to hear back from them. I never did.

However, I did hear back from a cruise ship recruiter, and an audition was set up for the show band. Maybe this wasn't the end of ship life for me after all. I knew the show band was all reading, so I really hit the books. I started working on reading charts, and I really focused on playing jazz. This was my weak spot. I started listening to and practicing along with every jazz record I could get my hands on. It was a good time. I was able to practice six to ten hours a day. I was reading charts and playing along with all the great jazz and big band drummers of our time like Buddy Rich, Gene Krupa, Brian Blade, and Jeff Hamilton. I brushed up on my traditional Latin grooves and this proved to be exceptionally useful.

The audition process for the show band is notably interesting. On the day of the audition, you receive an email with music charts attached to it. You get thirty minutes to print out the charts and look them over. Then you get a call from the recruiter and you have to perform whatever part of the charts they ask you to play. The audition is high speed, just like the gig. If you have a good enough audition, you get an email a few days later with an offer to join the show band on a cruise ship somewhere.

I was scheduled to join a ship in the Caribbean, and I couldn't wait to get back to ship life again. The ship I was assigned to would be sailing to St. Thomas, St. Martin, Puerto Rico, Jamaica, Cozumel, and Grand Cayman. These were all places I had never been. To me, the itinerary sounded like a perfect tour of the most beautiful islands in the world, with a stop by that island where I could finally get that offshore bank account I always wanted.

The cruise company flew me down to Miami. As far as drum gear went, all I had to carry along were my cymbals. This is a dream. Only having to carry cymbals and your drumsticks to a gig is a drummer's wet dream. Trust me, I've had nightmares about getting a gig in an eighties metal-band that required me to lug around one of those giant drum sets like you see in bands such as Van Halen or Pantera. That is a true nightmare.

I arrived in Miami around seven p.m., and I was exhausted. The hotel was nice, but it was in the older downtown section of Miami, which has all the charm of a homeless shelter with a crime rate equal to Michael Vick's backyard. I checked into the hotel room and immediately collapsed into the bed. I was asleep in seconds. However, I didn't stay asleep for long. I woke up when suddenly the door to my room flew open. I jumped up out of bed. A dark shadowy figure walked inside the room. I was positive I was going to die, and I hadn't even had the chance to buy a *Guayaba y Queso* pastry in downtown Miami yet. It is a cruel world sometimes indeed.

"Who the hell are you?" I yelled towards the shadow in the doorway. I could see that he had some luggage in his hand. I thought he was about to race out of the room with my cymbals and bow ties. Instead he just froze.

"Is dis room 157?" He said. His voice was unmistakably Indian.

"Yes. This is my room. How did you get in here?"

"I am afraid dis is my room as well," he said very kindly and sheepishly. I looked at him. My eyes adjusted to the low light of the room, and then I understood what was going on.

"Are you a crew member?" I asked him.

"Yes, are you?"

"Are you serious? Those cheap bastards. Yes, I'm a crew member," I said. I rubbed my eyes and then looked around the room. There was only one bed. I looked back at my new roommate and gave him a puzzled look.

"There is only one bed in this room," I said, "and you're not sleeping in bed with me." He just turned around and left. The funny thing is that it didn't surprise me one bit that the cruise ship company would welcome me back to ship life by booking me in a single-bed hotel room with another male crew member. I took a deep breath. *Welcome back to ship life*, I thought.

Early the next morning, I took a shuttle bus to the ship. I walked up the rickety gangway and through the large opening on the side of the cruise ship. The Indian security guard, who looked as miserable as I remembered, pushed my bags through the outdated x-ray machine. I walked back onto the I-95 to find the same rushing city of internationals that I had left on the last ship, but with new faces running every which way. The forklifts were scooting through the crowd, beeping and scraping by, and only adding to the absolute chaos of the environment. That familiar odor of fresh paint, smoke, trash compactor, and body odor welcomed me at the door. *Ahhhh, it's great to be back.* And it absolutely was.

The music director, Ricky, was waiting to welcome me onboard and show me around the ship. First, we stopped by my room where my new roommate, a chunky bass player in the lounge band who looked and dressed as if he had completely given up on life, proceeded to give me the low down on the rules of what he apparently considered "his" room. He thoroughly exercised his inner-control-freak ways and king-of-the-hill complex in a matter of minutes. He frantically pointed around the room.

"This is my shit, and this is where you can put your shit. Don't touch my shit, and don't eat my food. I sleep after the gig, so there's not going to be any late night partying and no girlfriends over to spend the night or anything. Keep your shit off the floor, and clean the sink after you shave. Don't be all loud and shit when you come in at night, and don't smoke or drink in the room. I'm a recovering alcoholic, and I quit smoking last year, so I don't even want to smell the shit. Don't play the TV loud while I'm asleep or turn on the lights. If you come in at night, use a flashlight. I've got an extra one if you need it. I snore at night (which turned out to be a gross under-exaggeration. This guy transformed into a dump truck with a bad muffler after he fell asleep), so if you got a problem with it, use some ear plugs or something. You got two drawers here and half of this thing over here to store your clothes, so there is no reason why they should be on the floor. We got one chair and don't bring another one in. There's no room for it. This is where I keep my bass and my guitar, so don't put any of your shit there. I'm going to the crew mess. I'll be back in fifteen minutes or something." With that he walked out of the room. I looked at the music director and laughed.

"He's quite pleasant," I said.

"Well, he had his own room for a while. Now that you're here, he has to give it up and share. Having your own room is kind of a big deal, and besides that, he's kind of a jerk anyway. I'm trying to get you moved in with someone else. I think I got it worked out, but I have to get it approved by the staff captain. Just hang tight, and I'll see what I can do," Ricky said, and then he shrugged and motioned me out the door.

Ricky was right. Having your own room is a *big* deal on the ship. But let me put this into perspective. Finding a banana that is not rotten in the crew mess is a really big deal. Having a cook who puts chicken fingers on the menu two nights in a row is considered possibly to be an act of divine intervention. Getting your own room is *the* biggest deal on a ship. The only thing better than having your own room is when the ship's engine happens to have mechanical problems while the ship is docked in port, you have the night off and get to have an overnight stay in Aruba or Hawaii or Sydney or something, and it's a Saturday night and the bus to Bondi Beach is running all night long. That's how much of a big deal it is to have your own room. When you live and work in one of the most cramped, crowded, and chaotic environments on the planet, having your own room is the best thing in the world. You get your own space to get away, relax, stretch out, sleep when you want, and have your girlfriend over whenever you want to. Unfortunately, it hardly ever happens.

However, there are quite a few jobs you can get on a cruise ship that will practically guarantee that you will have your own room. If you are thinking about working on a cruise ship, then start taking notes or pull out that highlighter because these are the jobs you want. They include working as an officer, the captain, music director, dance captain, doctors, nurses, for some bizarre reason art auctioneers, and a few other positions high up in the ship hierarchy. The rest of the crew members have to share a room. Though, when you get a good roommate it can be way more fun than living alone.

Before I left my new room, I opened my suitcase and threw a few shirts on the ground just to annoy my jerk of a roommate. The guy had already gotten things off on the wrong foot. In my opinion, he deserved to have his obsessive-compulsive-disorder nipple tweaked a little bit. We left the room and walked a few hundred feet to the stage. Already, I could tell this ship was much nicer than the last one. My last ship with The Cat's Meow, the *Fantasy*, was built in 1982. That cruise ship definitely looked its age. This ship, though, was much newer and much cleaner. It had been built in 2000, and it was astoundingly larger. Cruise ships just continue to grow in size. The *Oasis*, owned by Royal Caribbean, can carry over 6,000 passengers.

Astoundingly, the *Oasis* is only slightly smaller than a Nimitz class aircraft carrier. This new ship I was on could hold just over 2,000 passengers. It looked massive.

We were standing backstage of the main theater. It was nearly pitch black, and it took a while for my eyes to adjust to the low light. Backstage there are black painted walls, a black stage floor, and black curtains. The curtains had these small, fiber-optic lights running through them that twinkled like stars against a pitch black sky. The theater was empty and the front curtain was open.

An empty theater is a magical place. The stage is perfectly still. The curtains twinkle. Spotlights illuminate the large expanse of the perfectly smooth stage that looks out on a towering auditorium of richly upholstered seats and metal rails that are polished to a gleaming shine. An empty stage is one of the few places where the infinite nature of possibility is most powerfully felt. An empty stage is yours. It is up to you to make of it what you can, and what you make of it will be reflected back at you in the number of filled seats, the applause of the crowd, and the satisfaction of the performance.

However, cruise ship musicians usually do not perform on the stage. Cruise ship musicians work in the pit. The pit is a small platform that is usually found in front of the stage. It is filled with music stands, cables, chairs, and a drum set off to one side. The pit is hydraulically powered so that it can be lowered and raised, and ninety percent of the time the platform of the pit is lowered down into a small, black box. This gives the performers on stage the full attention of the audience. The pit is a dark place. It is a black void. Also, on most ships, the musicians have to wear black when they perform. So, if you look down into the pit during a show, you are likely to see little lights shining onto piles of sheet music and a collection of floating heads and hands in the darkness.

We walked over to the pit, and Ricky handed me a folder that was two inches thick and practically bursting at the seams with sheet music.

"This is the show we're playing tonight, so give it a look and be ready at about seven o'clock," Ricky said. Sheet music was poking out of the sides of the dark blue folder. The edges of the sheet music were worn, frayed, and stained. The folder was packed with music charts for the production show.

A production show on a cruise ship is a nonstop, hour-long music performance. Everything you have to play is written out on the charts. All the breaks, complex transitions, difficult drum fills, segues, drum patterns, time signature changes, and set-ups for the horn section are all on the charts. And in just two hours, Ricky expected me to play everything on those charts perfectly.

"This is what we are playing two hours from now?" I asked and tried to conceal my concern as best I could.

"Yep," Ricky said.

All of this would become routine a few months from now. It would become routine to be given a book full of charts I had never laid eyes on just two hours, or thirty minutes, or two minutes before the performance. But, this was my first contract as a show band drummer, and this was not what I was used to. I was hardly accustomed to reading charts at all. Playing with bands back home, we would sometimes spend months getting shows together. We were practicing five or six hours a day for three or four days a week to put together a two-hour show. In college, the jazz band would spend two months rehearsing for a single show. In this situation, I would have somewhere between fifty and sixty hours to prepare for a single one-hour performance.

On the cruise ship, you usually have about twenty minutes of rehearsal time to prepare an hour long performance. It's amazing how fast the show band works. You have to know your parts before you even know what your part is going to be. In other words, you have to put your time in at the practice room. The performance doesn't need to be flawless for you to get by, but it does have to be played very well. Otherwise, you'll just drive everyone else in the show band banana cakes, and you'll also have the other musicians wishing they could hurl their saxophones, trombones, and drumsticks at the imaginary target on your head. I bet I've even had that imaginary target on my head a few times. Actually, I'm certain that I have (a certain trumpet player comes to mind).

"Let me show you the Aviom system, and then I'll let you look over the show," Ricky said. I had no idea what he was talking about. "The Aviom system," Ricky continued, "is that little blue box attached to your music stand." He pointed towards my stand. There was this box with knobs and buttons all over it. All eleven stands in the pit had an Aviom box attached to it.

"The Aviom is your own little control box. You can adjust the volume of each player in the band as well as the singers on stage. You can also adjust the volume of the metronome and the backing tracks. There are two backing tracks that guide the band through the shows. There is a backing track for the horn section and a backing track for the rhythm section. We all wear headphones when we play the shows, and you can hear the metronome, the band, the backing tracks, and the singers in your headphones. It's totally up to you as to how you adjust your Aviom. You just have to decide what you want to hear. I wouldn't recommend listening to the singers; they just throw you off. You definitely want the metronome, and you most likely will want to hear the backing track for the rhythm section in case you get lost in the show. But don't get lost or it will mess everybody up."

Got it. Don't screw up.

"Oh yeah, and you can't always trust the metronome. Sometimes it's wrong," Ricky said.

For the non-musicians who are reading this book, a metronome is a device that keeps perfect time. The sound is produced digitally and it can be whatever sound you want: a cowbell, a beep, a sound like the snapping of fingers, whatever. The metronome keeps time for the band during the production shows. Everything in the show is synched to the metronome— what the band plays, the lighting for the show, the moves the dancers make, and the set changes. This is how the cruise ships operate their production shows. This is how Broadway does it too. A lot of big-name pop acts even use a metronome in their in-ear headphones during their live shows.

"So, what do we do when the metronome is wrong?" I asked.

"You just have to play through it, and do the best you can do. You'll learn where the metronome is wrong and feel your way through it," Ricky said.

What Ricky wasn't telling me is that, in a lot of sections of the production shows, the metronome can be embarrassingly wrong, completely wrong, as wrong as possible. Imagine trying to play a song on an instrument flawlessly. It is quite hard to do. It takes most people years of practice to make the sounds they want to make on their instrument. Now imagine trying to play a song flawlessly at a certain predetermined tempo. This is even more challenging. Now imagine playing that song at that exact tempo, and play it flawlessly, while wearing headphones that are playing a ridiculously loud beeping sound that has no relation whatsoever to the tempo or feel of the song that you are flawlessly trying to perform. It is like trying to pat your head and rub your belly at the same time while hula hooping, jump roping, and painting an exact replica of the Mona Lisa using a paint brush between your teeth. It is ridiculous that the pre-recorded metronome in these production shows on cruise ships never get fixed. What it meant for me was that my job, a job that I was going to need a matrix-style infusion of information and skill to successfully execute, just became much more difficult.

"OK," was all I could say. I either had to do it, make it work and play this show, or lose the job. It was simple.

Through the five years I worked on the cruise ship, I had the opportunity to work in nearly all the types of bands that you find on a ship. The show band gig is completely different than any of the other music jobs at sea such as playing with the jazz trio in the cigar bars, or the lounge band in one of the clubs, or the reggae band out on the lido deck. For example, when you play in the lounge band, jazz trio, or the reggae band, you pretty much get your six to eight hours' worth of music together, and then play these same songs over and over again. Most of the reggae bands and lounge bands also don't use any actually written music. The exception is the jazz trio, yet even there you hardly ever read extremely detailed charts for tunes. That kind of ignores the whole spirit of jazz, a musical style rooted in expression, freedom, and improvisation.

Show band musicians are expected to be capable of playing every style of music. They have to be able to read music extremely proficiently, and even be capable of sight reading at a moment's notice. The show band not only performs for the production shows, but they also perform traditional jazz sets, Dixieland jazz shows, and pop sets with the production singers. The show band also is the backup band for all the different guest singers that perform on each cruise. This is one of the more interesting gigs for the show band. When the guest singers arrive on board, the show band usually has about twenty or thirty minutes to rehearse before performing an hour long show in front of a crowd of a thousand or more passengers. It's fast paced. You must be prepared for anything and have full throttle focus. And the result can be incredible when every player in the band is really locked into their instrument, focused, and prepared for the performance. There is nothing that can bring the full power of music to the stage like a solid rhythm section absolutely locking into a tight groove and having a phenomenal seven-piece horn section lay blistering and precise horn arrangements on top.

In fact, the cruise ship is one of the last places where a musician still has the opportunity to play with a big band like this. Granted, there are a few big bands still touring around the country like the ghost band of the Glen Miller Orchestra, and you can still get your kicks in the community big bands and with the college jazz bands. Also, in most big cities you can find one or two wedding bands with a full seven-piece horn section, but these types of gigs are rare these days. For the most part, the problem is that there just isn't enough money to keep these big bands going, so they have become an endangered species in the musical world.

Even the cruise ships in recent years have cut their big bands back to a pathetic size in an effort to save the cruise companies money. As a result, most of the show bands on cruise ships aren't really *big* bands anymore, and it's a shame to see those big horn sections just dwindle in size. When I first started working on the ships, the show band had two trumpets, a tenor sax, an alto sax, a baritone sax, and two trombones. The horn section had this fat, dynamic, full, and powerfully complex sound. It was incredible what the band could do with charts that were arranged for these full horn sections. The drum chair is exceptionally fun when you're setting up the hits and supporting the melodies of a full horn section like this. The show bands on a cruise ship used to really kick.

Over the years, I watched the horn section dwindle down to three horns—a trumpet, a sax, and one trombone. In the worst scenarios, the entire horn section has been canned, and the ship hires a keyboard player to play the horn lines. It's a big loss for the cruise ships whether they realize it yet or not. Music is an integral part of the cruising experience, and the music just isn't the same without that full horn section. A twelve-piece band creates a prestigious setting for a cruise, as well as an environment of tradition, class, status, and exclusiveness for passengers. This can never be accomplished with the small bands that are on stage now. Also, from a technical music perspective, having a three-piece horn section often creates real trouble when a band is trying to read horn parts that were originally written for a much larger horn section. The disappearance of the horn sections on cruise ships is a real loss, and I am advocating here for the cruise ships to bring the band back. Restore the horn section to an effective, respectable, and valuable size. Bring the band back.

Back on stage, I had two hours to rehearse before show time. I had a million questions for the rest of the band about how the shows worked, about the Aviom system, about everything. But on the ship there's not a lot of help. Most of the other guys in the pit have done these production shows hundreds, if not thousands of times, and it is just part of the hazing process to see how bad you screw everything up, and then give you a hard time about it. Besides, there is a very low retention rate on the ships, and remarkably high turnover in the show band. There are always new musicians joining the ship and screwing everything up in the pit, fumbling around on their instrument like they've never played before. So, the band generally takes on an apathetic and unapologetic attitude toward the F-N-G.

I was seated next to the bass player. The keyboard player was in front of me. It was crammed tight. I looked over at the bass player. He was a husky, Hawaiian looking guy with a square jaw and a crew cut like a marine. He was practicing an up-tempo jazz section in the show.

"Hey, how does the show start?" I asked. The bass player just kind of looked at me, effectively gave me the most confused looked he could, complete with one eye brow lifted up, and then turned towards Ricky who was tuning up his sax.

"Hey Ricky," The bass player gave a small laugh under his breath, "the F-N-G wants to know how the show starts."

As soon as the bass player said "F-N-G", the rest of

the band stopped their tuning and warm-up routines. It was like stopping a record. I could hear the scratching sound in my head, as most of the band turned and looked at me. They had all been introduced to me earlier in the day when I was getting shown around the ship. There were rushed introductions, and everyone I met had been very welcoming. However, now everyone was just kind of staring at me, and they all looked very concerned. I was left there thinking, *what the hell does F-N-G mean?* One of the guys in the band answered my question. He turned and looked at Ricky.

"Our drummer is a fucking new guy? The head office gave us a fucking-new-guy drummer? What the fuck? No offense to you Josh, but an F-N-G drummer has a lot to learn, and they are usually put on smaller ships to learn the ropes. You got thrown in here with a bunch of guys who have been doing this gig for a long time. We'll cut you some slack though. Good luck." He pulled his trumpet to his lips, shook his head, and muttered under his breath, "fucking new guy."

Now that my confidence had been completely obliterated, and my idea of a warm welcome had been entirely redefined, I looked to Ricky for some help on how the show was supposed to start. Ricky's response was mind-numbing. He talked at 90 miles an hour.

"I'll point at you, and you do a drum roll on the floor tom. While you're rolling, they will introduce the music director, and then I'll count off the band for the first chart in your book. The music director will call some people on stage, and we will play "St. Thomas" while they walk up to the stage. They are going to do a comedy bit, and then we will play the *Flintstone's* theme song. When I count it off, I will count in double time, and we are going to swing it really fast, so be ready. Then we'll play "St. Thomas" and then the *Rocky* theme song at the end of the Cruise Director's spiel. At this point put on your headphones. After a few minutes, I'll point at you to do the roll on the floor tom again, and then you will hear a voice in your headphones that will count off the show. That is the signal to start the first page of the production show. Got it?"

"Sure," I said. I was completely confused.

This is the nature of the drum chair in the show band. You will have a banjo player with a million cues in his show bark long detailed instructions at you ten minutes before you perform his show. The banjo player will, with a completely straight face, tell you to remember that when he plucks the fifth string on his banjo for the third time, during the second song of the fourth routine, you are supposed to hit your bass drum six times and then shout at him, "Hey, who stole my banjo!" or something ridiculous. It's high speed, and when you're the F-N-G there is a lot to learn. And you must learn it fast.

The show started. Ricky pointed at me. I performed a roll on the floor tom and stopped when the cruise director came out on stage. The cruise director managed to be entirely uninspiring and unentertaining with his collection of fart humor and jokes about how loud cruise ship toilets are when you flush them. Somehow, I made it through the pre-show routine of my first production show, with all of the finger pointing, cues, fast tempo *Flintstone's* theme and all. I put on my headphones. The music director pointed to me. I did a big roll on the low floor tom again, and then I felt the ship list a little to one side. The ship had left port a few hours before the show. Just before the production show, I could feel that we had moved into more open water. I could feel the waves picking up.

On a cruise ship, rough seas often make a drummer's job more difficult. You see, drummers are basically balancing on their drum chairs. Both legs essentially hover over the two pedals that their feet operate. When the seas are high, a drummer's balance is thrown off, and your sense of space is thrown off as well. Drumming requires a lot of precise muscle movements. When the ship is rocking, the amount of force required to thrust a drumstick towards a drum changes depending on whether the ship is rocking forwards or backwards. This listing of the ship can really throw off a drummer's timing and perception of how much force they need to use at any given movement. A new drummer on a cruise ship often has a difficult time adjusting to this new challenge. For me, the rocking of the ship was only making my job more difficult.

I continued to roll on the floor tom. I looked up towards the opening of the pit and saw a bright glow as the stage exploded with light. It was show time. I listened to my headphones for the cue. I glanced at the sheet music on the stand, hoping it was arranged in order. There was no time for mistakes. I fiddled with the Aviom system, readjusting a few volume knobs for the backing tracks, and checking to make sure the vocalist channel was off as Ricky had suggested. I intently listened, and then I heard a voice come through my headphones.

"One-two-three-four-one-two-ready-play." The hydraulic platform began to move upward as the band energized the room with the opening sequence of the show. The band was lifted out of the pit and placed in full view of the towering audience that filled the theater. The curtain opened behind us. In my peripheral vision, I could see a group of scantily clad female dancers wrapped in feather boas. They wore feather headdresses and were bouncing around the stage. From that moment, the show was nonstop.

Playing a production show is not like a bar gig or any other type of music performance. Usually, a band plays a song and then stops before they move on to the next one. However, a production show on a cruise ship is often one big medley, a near seamless flow of music. The band will often play the main verse and chorus of a tune, and then immediately go into the next song. For example, in just five minutes during a Motown style production show on a cruise ship, the band might play a seamless medley of "I Heard it Through the Grapevine," "Signed, Sealed, Delivered," "Let's Get it On," "Ain't too Proud to Beg," "Ain't No Mountain High Enough," and "Dancing in the Street." And the show will keep going like this without a break for an entire hour. Meanwhile, the musicians are ripping the sheet music from their stands and quickly reading the notes as they go by. At the end of the show, I was drenched in sweat and surrounded by sheet music that I had thrown onto the floor of the pit.

For the show finale, the band played through a version of Lionel Richie's "Dancing on the Ceiling." During this section of the show, the dancers grouped into pairs. They skillfully twirled, kicked, and jumped in perfectly synchronized movements. Occasionally, the dancers would turn towards the band and look into the pit and make a distractingly funny face at the band to try and throw us off. The lights flashed across the faces of the audience, musicians, and dancers as the ship slowly rocked back and forth.

Performing in a band is a great feeling, but there is nothing like working in a band with a cast of dancers and singers. It is a unique and extremely powerful force. The band provides the dancers with a rhythmic and emotional musical platform to express themselves, while the dancers visually bring the musicians' expressions to life. When I would perform in the production shows, I would look out across the stage and see the effect of the music seemingly ripple and spread out from the drum set and the rest of the show band. I would watch the dancers on stage react and express the music. They would illustrate the energy of youth and celebrate life through their skilled and beautiful movements. Then I would watch as the audience reacted to the entire performance. It was incredible.

Back in the pit, the band hit the final note, and the curtain closed. The dancers clapped to celebrate another well performed and injury-free performance. My own performance, while injury free, was far from well performed. I had nearly avoided serious disaster many times during the show, and I realized this was going to be a long road. The show band gig turned out to be a one-way street that led straight to the practice room for hours on end.

In the show band, every day is something new. One night we are in the theater with the dancers and singers ripping through charts and sweating under the lights in the main theater, and then the next day we are in one of the smaller clubs swinging traditional jazz for a cocktail hour. Then we're back in the theater backing up an accordion player performing the greatest collection of polkas ever assembled while riding a unicycle, or a heavy metal banjo player or something. And I tell you, you have not lived until you have played a banjo version of the theme song to *Jesus Christ Super Star* on a cruise ship. In the show band, you never know what the day might bring.

Performing in the show band was a ride on a great ocean highway that led to the most beautiful islands and beaches around the world, and a road filled with life-long friends from across the globe. Musicians often forge very deep friendships. During my first contract, there were some guys in the band that were F-N-G's like me. We experienced being told that there was a bowling alley on the bottom deck of the ship, only to go down there and find the laundry room and five Filipinos telling us to get the hell out of there. We experienced ship life together for the first time, and it created lifelong friendships.

Joining a band is an automatic pass into a fraternity. A band is a group of like-minded individuals that come from the same background, have gone through the same struggles, and have had the same strange and unexplainable compulsion to practice their instrument obsessively for hours and hours on end for years and years. As a result of this, musicians have developed the same neurotic, spastic, intense personality that every other musician has developed. It is a fraternity of people that, for whatever tragic or complex reason, have the same insatiable desire to receive an abnormal amount of attention and find themselves searching for a stage and a spotlight where they can be the star of their own show.

A band is a group of people who are all working towards the same goals to entertain, play great music, and to have fun. And as the ship rolls from port to port and from beach to beach, when you get a group of attention seeking, neurotic, and extraverted musicians on a slow boat to China, Bora Bora, New Zealand, Grand Cayman, Mexico, Alaska or wherever the ship is headed, you can bet one thing. You can bet that the time you spend on that cruise ship is going to be a lot of fun.

8

WHAT IS THE WORST PART ABOUT WORKING ON A CRUISE SHIP?

There are two words that all crew members despise with all of their rum-soaked hearts—Red Alert. Just whispering those two words into the ear of any crew member is enough to make them simultaneously cringe, get sick right where they are standing, and send them running to the nearest rail for a leap overboard. Whether the waters are shark- infested is of no concern in this matter. When a crew member is in the middle of a red alert, resting blissfully in the belly of a great white shark can sound like a better fate than what they have to endure. Suffering through red alert is worse than sitting through a Jersey Shore marathon. It is comparable to the pain one would endure if forced to watch back-to-back *Jersey Shore* marathons, which effectively makes it the seventh level of hell or something like that.

So, what is red alert? Red alert is a state of emergency that a cruise ship activates when 2 percent or more of the passengers or crew members on board contract a contagious sickness, and this happens much more than you would think. Let's explore how, shall we? First off, a cruise ship is a very cramped and crowded place. They are a playground paradise for viruses, germs, colds, and all sorts of little bugs that can make you sick. Let's put this into perspective. There are usually around 2,000 or more passengers and 1,000 crew members all packed onto the same ship. The law of averages makes certain that nine times out of ten, one of these passengers or crew members is going to walk up that gangway and climb right aboard that ship with a big stupid grin and be sick as a dog. Someone at some time is going to walk on board while they are right in the middle of an episode that has forced them to become more intimately engaged with their toilet than anyone should ever be. And when they climb aboard the cruise ship, they absolutely ruin the party for everyone else.

Cruise ships are where germs go to thrive. They are a germ's special little place, where there is always another full belly for the germs to fester and wreak unlimited havoc. On a ship, everyone is touching the same polished rails, sneezing and coughing into the same circulated air, sitting in the same chairs, sipping out of the same glasses, working out in the same gym, and swimming in the same pools and hot tubs. No legion of Filipino crew members armed with bottles of generic disinfectant spray and wash rags can always defeat these ubiquitous, stubborn, resilient bastards. No amount of scrubbing, cleaning, painting, spraying, wiping, rubbing, and polishing can win the war against the germs, especially when you are dealing with a cruise ship's arch nemesis, the industry's embattled foe—the norovirus.

The norovirus is one bad mother. When someone brings the virus on board, all they have to do is touch a pinky to a glass table, and the glass surface becomes a virus jungle—a Petri dish gone wild. Norovirus spreads so fast and so effectively from person to person, that the United States Center for Disease Control (the CDC) considers it to be the leading cause of food-borne disease outbreaks in the country, and the norovirus is without a doubt the leading cause of viral outbreaks on cruise ships. This makes the virus, without a doubt, the cruise industry's worst enemy. The norovirus is just gross. It's also a part of a larger group of similar viruses called Norwalk-like viruses (that name just seems to add an apt level of creepiness to the sound of the sickness, doesn't it?).

If you are unlucky enough to contract the norovirus, you will know it fairly quickly. The virus causes what the CDC calls acute gastroenteritis. In other words, you develop an extreme case of diarrhea, vomiting, stomach pain, and general nausea. And believe me, the last thing you want on a cruise ship is extra help with nausea. This is especially the case when sailing through twenty-foot seas in the South China Sea, Tasman Sea, or while skirting the outer edge of a hurricane in the Caribbean. Trust me. People can hardly walk down the corridors without clutching a puke bag in one hand during these unfortunate cruises. If you add norovirus to the equation, the ship becomes nothing less than a bobbing cesspool of sickness.

Norovirus isn't all of your worries on a cruise ship though. I remember one particular cruise when the ship stopped in Vietnam and picked up some particularly special spinach that just happened to be infested with the intestinal parasite called cyclospora. You are never so much aware that the human body is capable of such acts of fluid loss until you meet the very unfriendly cyclospora. If there ever was someone that should be given the official title of the world's most effective party pooper, it is a cruise ship crew member or passenger that contracts norovirus or cyclospora. And on a ship, these parasites and viruses spread fast.

To help combat these unwanted cruise critters there is a color-coded alert system that has been put in place aboard cruise ships. The lowest alert level is called green alert. During a green alert, the ship is a happy place where the crew members conduct a normal level of sanitation, and all eating areas are open for passengers and crew. The ship will activate the more serious yellow alert if two or three passengers or crew members aboard a cruise ship show up at the ship's clinic with symptoms of norovirus or other threatening sicknesses. Yellow alert is fairly common. Under yellow alert, ship passengers and crew members are required to use hand sanitizer before entering food serving areas, the cleaning crews are kicked up a notch, chlorine content in the cleaning solutions is boosted, and the ship begins to adopt a smell similar to a massive swimming pool.

However, sometimes this just isn't enough. Sometimes the norovirus, or whatever else happens to be spreading on the ship, wins the battle against the cleaning crew and infects more than 2 percent of the passengers and crew members on board. This is the magic number. It may seem like a small amount of people, but remember that most ships have 3,000 or more people on board. So, when 2 percent of the passengers and crew aboard the ship are sick, there are more than sixty people walking around infecting everyone else. The virus spreads fast when you have sixty people spraying entire colonies of norovirus in every direction. This is considered an outbreak, and this is when the dreaded, dismal, and horrid red alert is activated.

This is the exact time when you want to act fast and get the hell off that ship. These are my directions for you:

1) In complete secrecy, gather a group of your most trusted and reliable friends. Choose wisely. It is preferred to select those with military skills, navigation abilities, or friends that are just plain crazy. Experience handling small watercraft is a plus. Choose one

expendable person that you don't necessarily like to come along with you. We will codename this person "The Pawn." He or she will come in handy at a later date.

2) Dress in all black. Judas Priest T-shirts are fine, or you can find a group of show band musicians and steal their clothes. They always wear black, and they are usually easy to find. They are probably drinking in the crew bar. If you do not find them there, then check their beds. When they are not drinking, they are usually sleeping.

3) Head to the midnight buffet and fill your backpacks with as many bottles of water and chicken fingers as they can hold. Do not, I repeat *do not*, forget the honey mustard sauce. This is very, very good.

4) Find a social host and force them to tell you the location of the storage room for the cheap champagne on the cruise ship. Waterboarding may be required. This is acceptable. However, repetitively ridiculing their poor stage presence usually does the trick. Go to the champagne storage room and take as many bottles as possible. Just for good measure, kidnap the social host. They know lots of bad cruise ship jokes and are really good at calling bingo. This will definitely come in handy during the long voyage ahead.

5) Under the cover of darkness, and while nearly everyone on the cruise ship is sleeping, seize control of

a lifeboat. Make sure to leave "The Pawn" aboard the virus-infected ship. "The Pawn" must lower you safely onto the surface of the calm Caribbean Sea. Now paddle, paddle, paddle as fast as you can! Paddle like the rising of the sun depends on it, until you reach a beautiful beach where you can feast on your chicken fingers, drink your cheap champagne, and play bingo as everyone else aboard the cruise ship faces the wrath of the red alert. You can thank me later.

While the above may be written in the spirit of fun and humor, the red alert is no laughing matter for a cruise ship crew member. If crew members or passengers contract the norovirus, they are quarantined. There are no exceptions. The cruise that you paid for could be happening during your honeymoon or your Grandmother's hundredth birthday party, and you will still be quarantined. If you get sick during a red alert, you're on lock down. You can't leave your room for anything. Your cabin steward will deliver your daily rations on a plastic hospital tray that includes Alka-Seltzer, Jell-O, crackers, and, if you're lucky, a bowl of chicken broth. You'll be lucky if you can stomach anything at all. Most likely you will spend the next five days living off of Alka-Seltzer and Tylenol. It's the pits. Getting sick on a cruise ship is even worse when you're a passenger and you paid hundreds or even thousands of dollars to come on a cruise only to contract the norovirus and become unbearably ill.

If you ever find yourself with the norovirus or cyclospora, or something like this, my advice is to cover the room wall-to-wall with plastic. Tape the seams. Lie down in the middle of the room, and start a slow drip with enough horse tranquilizers to keep you comatose, unconscious, and completely oblivious to what is happening around and inside of you for at least the next five days. Spend the time you would have spent pleading for your life to end in this safe, little, plastic-wrapped room dreaming about the Dallas Cowboy Cheerleaders running in slow motion, or being trapped with Mathew McConaughey on an island with no T-shirts, or whatever it is that you dream about. When you wake up, roll up your filthy plastic wrap, take a shower, stash the horse tranquilizer drip for next cruise, and move on with your life.

The worst part about red alert for a passenger is that the buffets are closed. That's right, I know that a cruise without buffets sounds like an oxymoron, but the cruise companies actually do it. Worse still is the fate the crew suffers. When it is red alert, the crew can no longer be in passenger areas, and they close our buffets too. Now, I've already thoroughly explored the fact that the food in the crew mess is probably as close to dog food as can legally be served to a human, and I am sure you think the food could not possibly get worse. Yet, it does indeed. I have become almost entirely convinced that the cruise companies have used the implementation of red alert as an excuse to transform the cruise ship into something that closely resembles medieval torture. The transformation would be complete if they brought out two horses to draw and quarter, a colorful collection of cat-of-nine-tails, and a row of pillories. During a red alert, crew members are served possibly the blandest and most unpalatable food possible, which sadly isn't that much different from what is usually served in the crew mess, now that I think about it.

During one particularly terrible red alert, crew members were served nothing but noodles with olive oil and an assortment of bread rolls for an entire week straight. Eating nothing but noodles with olive oil and bread rolls for anything longer than a couple of days is enough to drive you mad on its very own. Crew members are also only permitted to leave the crew area for work. This means that apart from the crew deck, crew members must stay in the all-tan, crowded, stuffy, cheap-motel looking, stinky, poorly-lit confines of the crew area. Put on top of that the fact that crew members have someone at all hours of the day barking orders at you and forcing you to wash your hands every time you even so much as look at the bread rolls, and you have a situation that will drive even the most strong-willed individuals completely banana-cakes insane. To this day, I'm not convinced that the cruise company's reasoning is sound. And I firmly believe that the individual who came up with the guidelines as to how crew members are treated during red alert should be examined for complete inaptitude and absolute stupidity. It is simply common sense that feeding an entire crew nothing but noodles and bread rolls for a week is an absolutely ineffective way to boost the immune system which could save crew members from contracting the prevalent virus that is lurking in every nook and cranny of the cruise ship. If you find yourself on a cruise ship and you so much as hear a rumor about red alert—run. For Pete's sake, save yourself and run. You don't want to go where that ship is sailing, especially if you're a crew member.

And the fun doesn't stop with the norovirus and cyclospora. There is an entire legion of communicable viruses, parasites, and diseases that together comprise the worst part of working on a cruise ship. In the honorable mention category for the worst sicknesses you can contract on a cruise ship are the common flu, Legionnaires' disease, E. coli, salmonella infantis, and salmonella typhi, which is commonly known as typhoid. In 1996, 330 passengers aboard an Italian ship cruising in the Mediterranean contracted severe cases of shigella dysenteriae, probably as a result of eating contaminated cod or swordfish. In 1989, seventy-two passengers and twelve crew members developed shigella flexneri. The company determined it was most likely a result of eating German potato salad. And then there are cases of staphylococcus aureus contracted from raspberries, vibrio cholerae from Asian rice, SRSV from contaminated bathrooms, and all sorts of nasty bacteria and viruses from eating seafood and meats.

There have even been several deaths as a result of these food poisonings, as well. One minute you're sitting on the lido deck with a big silly grin on your face, watching islands float by at sunset while stuffing down heaping spoonfuls of German potato salad, and then the next day you're searching for horse tranquilizers because some mindless dolt forgot to put the mayonnaise back in the refrigerator, or wash the spinach, or rinse the raspberries. It happens. Believe it. It's true. I'd say you should do what the kings of old used to do. Buy an extra ticket for the cruise, and bring a food tester along with you. If your food tester gets sick, for god's sake, don't eat it. So, if you ever hear the words "red alert" then paddle, paddle, paddle, man!

There isn't much that you can experience aboard a cruise ship that comes close to the horror of the red alert, but there are a few things that come close. The air quality on a ship is one of them. Passengers don't have to worry about this so much. Passengers all have nice air filters in their rooms. If you're ever in a passenger room on a cruise ship, just look up. Those fancy little boxes that are plugged into the ceiling are cleaning the air at least enough so that it doesn't smell really bad. Hopefully, they are cleaning the air enough so that it is healthy to breathe too. Unfortunately, on many cruise ships most of the crew members don't have air filters. We don't have nifty little boxes in our ceilings. Instead, we have holes. There is a tan cover over this hole with a little dial on it that hardly ever works. This dial is intended to enable a crew member to increase or decrease the amount of air that is coming out of this hole, but it is just a hole nonetheless. And the quality of the air that comes out of this hole in the ceiling can smell terrible. The air can smell so bad that it is routine for crew members to stuff fabric-softener sheets into these holes just to mask the horrible smell of the air that is pumped into their rooms. This is a very common practice on cruise ships. I've even had some of my cabin stewards stuff the holes with fabric-softener sheets without me asking them to.

What you have to understand is that the air is circulated throughout the cruise ship. Sure, the air is pulled inside of the ship from outside, but that air sometimes has to circulate through quite a few rooms before it arrives at a crew member's cabin. Now, let me be clear though. I am not an engineer. I will not to pretend to know with certainty how these ventilation systems function and specifically how they work. What I believe is simply my opinion. I have only made inferences from the observations I have made of this situation. Now, with that disclaimer out of the way, let's continue. There is a seemingly endless chain of crew quarters that the air on a cruise ship must pass through before it arrives at your crew cabin. So, everyone in a way is breathing the same air on the ship, and sometimes the air that is pumped into the ship from outside isn't very clean to begin with. If the wind is blowing hard and blowing the wrong way, then the wind may blow some of that dark smoke that constantly billows from the ship's funny-shaped smokestack right into the intake vents that suck the air into your cabin. This is not funny at all when you have to breathe it. And if someone is smoking a cigarette a few cabins down from your crew quarters, then you are going to be smoking that cigarette too. If the outdoor designated crew smoking section just happens to be right in front of the intake vent that sucks the air into your crew cabin, (and this appears to actually happen) then you are smoking all of those cigarettes too. And almost everyone smokes on a cruise ship, and they are allowed to smoke in their cabins.

Thankfully, the cruise ship companies have gotten better over the years about the problem of exposing crew members to secondhand smoke. Just a few months ago, I read somewhere that several cruise lines were going to ban smoking in all indoor areas on their cruise ships with an exception of the cigar bar. In my opinion, this is a wonderful thing. If those who choose to smoke cigarettes must smoke, let them do it outside where they are not affecting everyone else's health (that is, unless they are smoking in front of an intake vent). However, when I first started working on cruise ships, crew quarters looked like a scene from a Quentin Tarantino film. Everyone was smoking everywhere. The smoke was so thick that the crew area looked like a 1970's bar at last call. The official smoking policy, at least as I remember it, at that time stated that you shouldn't smoke while lying in bed because you might fall asleep and start a fire. The policy also stated that you *could* smoke in your room as long as your roommate was fine with it, but if you smoked in your room you had to stand up or sit in a chair or something. The problem is that when a crew member smokes cigarettes in their crew cabin, the smoke doesn't only affect that crew member's roommate. The smoke travels through the ventilation system. Therefore, the smoke seems to travel to all of the other cabins that are connected to the cabin where the cigarette smoke originated. Cigarette smoke is probably still a problem on cruise ships. Right now, there are crew members who are sitting on their bed while they watch smoke just pour into their cabin through the hole in their ceiling.

And while the cruise ship companies have changed the rules regarding smoking over the years for the better, these rules on many ships are rarely enforced. When the cruise lines first announced that they were changing their smoking rules that applied to crew members, and that crew members could no longer smoke in their rooms, the response was absolute apathy. No one changed. No one cared. No one enforced the no-smoking policy. I remember bringing up this problem at a meeting where we were encouraged to vent our frustrations and bring up any issues that concerned us.

"I have smoke just pouring into my cabin from my vent because other people are smoking in their cabins. What should I do about this?" The cruise director just kind of gave me a blank stare like I was a complete idiot. This particular cruise director must have had the IQ of a boiled hot dog and was moodier than a pit bull on steroids. She had more wrinkles around her lips than the Queen of England, mostly a result of a lifetime of chain smoking. She just looked at me and then after lengthy consideration, which was probably the amount of time it took for her brain to process simple information, she said one the most idiotic things anyone has ever said to me.

"Well," she put her hands on her hips for some sort of authoritarian effect. "I think this cruise ship is my home. I think you should be able to do whatever you want in your own home. So, if people want to smoke in their own home, then they should be allowed to do it." *So, this is what happens when morons control a cruise ship.* This line of logic was more of an egregious breach of reason than McCarthyism. Paula Abdul could have made a more sensible and understandable argument than that. But she was in control. She put her hands back on her hips, stared right at me, squinted her eyes, channeled her inner Wicked Witch of the West, and said, "I don't think this is something you really want to fight, on this ship anyway."

I decided to fight it, and it turned out she was right. I made an appointment with the staff captain, so I could talk to him directly and diplomatically about the issue. The staff captain is as high up the hierarchy in the chain of command that a crew member can go without speaking directly to the captain of the ship. The staff captain is the person who really has the power to make changes on the ship for the crew, and there are a lot of great staff captains out at sea. There are many incredible cruise directors, staff captains, and captains that I admire and respect very deeply for their professionalism, skill, dedication, and excellence at their job. However, on this ship it turned out that this was not the case at all. They were idiots. I showed up to the staff captain's office in high spirits and knocked on the door.

"Come in," the staff captain or someone on the other side of the door said. I opened the door and could not believe what I saw. Behind a large wooden desk was the staff captain. He had an officer on each side of him, and all three of them were smoking cigarettes in this tiny office where I had come to ask for help about the problem of people smoking on the ship. I felt I knew right away what was going on.

"What is this all about?" I asked the staff captain directly. Diplomacy was out the porthole window at this point.

"I'm not-ah sure-ah what you mean-ah by that-ah?" the staff captain said in his barely understandable accent. He pulled hard on his cigarette and blew the smoke up into the cloudy air. I was livid.

"What I mean is that, as you well know, I came to talk to you about the problem of crew members smoking in undesignated crew areas, and all three of you are smoking here. This is ridiculous."

"I don't-ah know what you mean-ah," the staff captain leaned forward and looked right at me. He stood up and walked over to me with the cigarette in his hand. "I don't-ah see anyone-ah smoking here-ah," he took a deep drag of his cigarette and blew the smoke right in my face. *So, this is what happens when idiotic assholes control a cruise ship.*

As if on cue, the Wicked-Witch-of-the-West cruise director emerged from her cabin. She looked like the Grinch with a big wrinkled grin on her face, and of course she was smoking a cigarette too. She gave me that same squinted look and said, "I don't think this is something you really want to fight, on this ship anyway." Unbelievable. I walked out of the room, slammed the door behind me, and left all three idiots in their smoke chamber. I could hear them laughing as I walked away. So, you can imagine how happy I was when I heard that many cruise ship companies have finally announced that they will no longer permit smoking inside the crew areas. Bravo. Now, all they have to do is actually enforce it.

Here would be the appropriate place to note that officers, staff captains, and anyone else who is of officer status on ships, don't simply have a hole in their ceiling. Officers have air filters and a convenient thermostat in their rooms to control the temperature at the touch of a button. The crew members get the holes. The crew members get the smoke, exhaust, body odor, and the farts that circulate from one room to the next. The crew members get the filth.

Almost equally as frustrating as the air quality on a cruise ship is the fact that crew members have to share a room. Getting a new roommate is like playing roulette, the odds are extremely high that you are going to lose. Walking onto a new ship and meeting your new roommate is always an interesting experience. Many times you are going to be stuck working and living with this person for months on end, and you will have to share a ten-by-ten foot room with a four-by-four foot bathroom. Getting a new roommate is hit or miss, and you usually know it right away if you lost or won. For example, I knew it was an absolute miss with the tired-of-life bass player during my first show band contract. However, I had never known with all my heart that I had lost miserably at the roulette table of cruise ship roommates, as the time I walked onto the ship for my fourth contract.

I walked down the hallway and went through the list in my head of things I did not want my roommate to be:

1) A drunk. There are an exceptionally high number of drunks out at sea. We are sailors for God's sake. Being a drunk is almost expected. Besides, there is cheap booze, a huge amount of time to kill, nowhere to go when the cruise ship is out at sea, and nearly always a party in the crew bar. So, most people decide they might as well drink. And it can be fun. However, having a drunk for a roommate gets old really fast when you have a roommate that stumbles into your cabin every night at four in the morning, hootin' and hollerin' about his lame escapade at the disco, and decides it is going to be acceptable and hilarious to throw crew-mess salami at your face while you're sleeping. Unfortunately, sometimes you will have to live with this roommate for more than six months. You can be pushed over the edge fairly quickly when you have to share room for six months with a drunk whose breath smells like a Jack Daniels distillery at one in the afternoon.

2) A smoker. Sometimes having a smoker as a roommate isn't that bad. There are plenty of considerate smokers. But this is a gamble as well. Many times, you end up living with a smoker that asks you if they may smoke in the room. When you tell him no, he does this thing where he stands half way out the door and blows the smoke into the hallway, as if this makes

the situation any better.

3) The depressed guy that never leaves the room. Cruise ships can be fun, but they can be lonely and depressing places for some people as well. Some crew members have a hard time coping when they only get a few hours of sunlight every day, are isolated from their family and friends, must eat food like chicken beak soup in the crew mess, and have to live under strict and often petty rules. Ship life can send some crew members into a downward spiral of depression, and sometimes they turn into people who never leave the room. They just sleep and sleep and sleep in the darkness until it is time to work. When you have a roommate like this, you can barely use the room. You're pretty much forced to just wander around the ship during the day or find a normal crew member that will let you hang out in their room.

4) The control freak. We have all had to deal with living with control freaks at some point in our lives. Nowhere is it more difficult to live with a control freak than on a cruise ship where you live in a ten-by-ten room. In a crew cabin, there is hardly enough room to walk around without crowding one another, nonetheless try and control. You know you're dealing with a control freak when your roommate is thrown into a frantic fit of rage because you moved his Darth Vader coffee mug from the *Star Wars* shelf to the *Battlestar Galactica* shelf.

5) The absolute freak. This is very common, as there are

plenty of absolute freaks on cruise ships. Once, I shared a room with a crew member who had the strangest sleeping habits I have ever experienced. He snored so loud he would wake *himself* up. His snoring was so loud it sounded like a chainsaw amplified by a megaphone. He would startle himself awake and cry for help as if that chainsaw was after him and set on severing his neck. He also had a Spanish girlfriend, so he was fluent in Spanish. He apparently would dream in Spanish and talk in his sleep in Spanish, except I wouldn't exactly call it talking. He would yell in his sleep, which would also startle him awake. Then he would let out a screeching yelp and begin yelling in Spanish as loud as he could. I didn't sleep a wink for nearly three days until I got transferred to another room.

6) The lifer. You find them in every line of work. They are employees that have no life outside of work, are completely obsessed with the office, and only talk about their jobs. They are the employees that are going to work at that job for the rest of their life. They are lifers, and you find plenty of them on cruise ships. You can always quickly identify these crew members because all they ever talk about is their last contract. All they ever talk about is their last ship.

"On my last ship, the dance cast was incredible."
"On my last ship, the food was way better."
"On my last ship, we had chicken fingers three days in a row once."

"On my last ship…"

"On my last ship…"

"On my last ship…"

Ahhhh! Someone tell them no one cares about their last fucking ship. It is awful to share a room with a lifer, with a "last ship-er."

Back in the hallway, I went over the list in my head of what I did not want in a roommate. I walked into my new room with loads of optimism. I crossed my fingers and hoped I wouldn't get a dumpy roommate. I walked into my new room. I heard some commotion coming from the bathroom to my right. When I looked into the bathroom, all of my fears were realized. It was one p.m. on a Sunday. My new roommate was hugging the toilet with drool hanging from one side of his mouth and a cigarette billowing smoke from the other. He was clutching a nearly empty bottle of Jack Daniels in one hand. He looked at me with half-open, bloodshot eyes. His eyes could not have been remotely close to working properly at this point.

"You must be Josh. I'm your new roommate," he said. The last part was said with a real chipper tone in his voice, as if I should be delighted. Then he puked in the toilet. The room was spotless, which was a sure sign of neat-freak tendencies, and there was a box of snoring strips sitting on the desk. I had lost miserably. About this time, an announcement came over the loud speaker in the ceiling of the room.

"Crew-ah member. Crew-ah member. Please-ah report-ah to your designated muster station-ah."

The boat drill was about to begin. My new roomy,

smelling like Hank Williams at a Christmas party, stumbled around the room and eventually donned his lifejacket in a tangled mess. He sloppily threw on his neon colored cap. The bill of the cap was cocked to one side. This made him look more like a member of the Beastie Boys than someone you would want to rely on while the ship is sinking, unless you wanted to have a last minute freestyle rap battle.

My roommate, looking like a drunken crew member version of Mike D., headed straight out the door towards his muster station. I was right behind him. I watched as he stumbled down the hallway and bumped into guests that were unenthusiastically attempting to form a line for the boat drill. He was fired that afternoon and walked down the gangway the next. He wasn't given a paid ticket home either. He had to figure it out for himself. He didn't care though. He had been on the ship for eight months straight and was very ready to go home. Eight months on a ship can do that to you. Believe it. It's true.

Boat drills are nearly as bad as the worst roommates. If you have ever cruised before, you know that the last thing you want to hear when you first board a cruise ship is an announcement telling you to put on your life jacket and go stand in the hot sun for half an hour, just so you can listen to an officer who can barely speak English tell you what you have to do if the boat crashes into an iceberg or into the coast of Italy. Yet, that is exactly what happens. Right after you get that first plate of chicken fingers, sip that first piña colada, or sink into a cushioned recliner by the pool, you are told to get up, stop relaxing, put down that ice-cold drink, and get your ass to the boat drill. Many of these passengers have traveled great distances and have experienced stressful voyages to get to the cruise ship. They have travelled across the country, or even across the world, with a vehicle full of whining children or with one whining spouse. When they finally board the cruise ship, all they want to do is relax. Instead, they are told to go immediately to the boat drill.

I believe that passengers, somewhere deep down in their hearts, know that the boat drills are necessary. However, passengers definitely know that boat drills are the pits. You only have to go on one cruise to develop an intense loathing for boat drills. So, imagine having to attend one of these boat drills every single week for months and months on end. And then imagine what it would be like to not just attend these boat drills, but to run them. Imagine having to deal with grumpy, tired, stressed out passengers at every single one of these boat drills. It can drive you mad. What you have to remember is that most people decide to go on a cruise because they are stressed out and need a vacation. These are the same people that have endured the stresses of an airport, or a Greyhound bus (God forbid), or a family car trip (even worse), not to mention the fiasco of parking at the gargantuan port and the mind numbing experience of waiting in that massive line to board the ship. These are the same people that show up to my boat drill. All of them are grumpy faced, full of attitude, and just looking for someone they can complain to about the stupid boat drill that could save their life. That's when they find me standing in my life jacket with a big goofy smile on my face and a bright neon hat on my head that reads, "CREW" in big black letters. The hat might as well read, "COMPLAIN HERE." And complain they do.

At a boat drill. there are always those two or three people that show up holding an enormous, dewy glass of frozen margarita, or the pudgy kid inhaling a massive bowl of chicken fingers, or the guy in the NASCAR hat sipping Bud Light through his mustache. They all get an attitude when you tell them they can't drink a big dewy glass of margarita, or drink Bud Light through their mustache, or eat bowls of chicken fingers at the emergency boat drill. None of them are happy when you have to take their drinks and food away from them.

A crew member's job at a boat drill is very simple, in theory. All you have to do is form the people who show up to your muster station into straight lines, and continue to form neat little rows of passengers as more arrive at the emergency drill. This sounds like it should be easy, right? However, at a boat drill there are always one or two rebellious and insubordinate nonconformists that refuse to get into the line. It's actually quite hilarious. It's just a boat drill, yet people will rebel...at the boat drill. It's mutiny on the ship. Some people just can't handle being told what to do, and they make life so hard for the measly crew member that is just trying to do his stupid job at the boat drill and move on with his life. You tell someone to stand in line so you can create a row of people in front of them, and the minute you turn your head, *Woop* (in a Chris Berman voice), they slip right back out of line and mess up the whole process. It's ridiculous, and the monotony of having to deal with these people and run a boat drill every single week can be enough to make you feel like you contracted norovirus every time you hear that boat drill announcement come over the loudspeaker in your crew cabin. For me, just the sight of a crew member in a life jacket is enough to trigger a complete nervous breakdown.

If I were ever asked to sum up what it is like to be a cruise ship crew member in four words or less I would say, "hurry up and wait." You hear this phrase constantly used on the ship. Crew members get rushed into a training room, meeting, a line, or to a drill, and then they sit and they wait...and wait...and wait, sometimes for hours, until whatever was so important to rush towards actually begins. The best (and therefore worst) example of the hurry up and wait phenomenon is immigration. Every time you board a new vessel, or leave the ship you were assigned to, you have to go through immigration. What this actually means is that all crew members are packed into one room, always very early in the morning, and then they have to sit and wait for hours and hours until the immigration officers arrive. To make matters worse, these immigration officers tend to process crew member's paperwork at a pace similar to the speed at which glaciers erode mountain ranges. It doesn't matter if you're Indian, Italian, English, or American. It doesn't matter what country you're "immigrating" back to. It doesn't matter if you're an American who is getting off the ship in America. You have to immigrate, and so you have to hurry up and get to immigration on time, and then wait, and wait, and wait. You have to hurry up and wait.

I remember sitting at immigration and just waiting and waiting. Two or three hours passed by, then a crew member just lost it. He was an American like me. I think he worked as a lighting technician in the main lounge or as a sound guy or something. He jumped up and started ranting and raving.

"What the hell is this?! Why are we sitting here waiting?! I am an American! Why am I at immigration?! Why do I have to immigrate to my own fucking country?"

Everyone else at immigration just sat there half asleep and ignored him. He just kept going. He went banana-cakes, was certifiable.

In fact, seeing crew members go bonkers really isn't that uncommon on the cruise ship. Ship life can be a very frustrating. I'm sure everyone goes bonkers for all kinds of reasons. Some of the crazy nervous breakdowns I have witnessed on a cruise ship probably have nothing to do with ship life at all. However, I am sure that many of them do.

I was riding on a crew elevator when a Food and Beverage manager stepped in and smiled at me. As soon as the elevator door closed, he turned around and started punching and kicking the metal walls, leaving big dents and yelling profanities the entire time. I remember one crew member who was constantly complaining about his life on the cruise ship. He was always quiet, but he looked *dark*. He looked like he needed a vacation. One night after he was drinking very heavily at the crew bar, I woke up to hear someone just screaming and ranting from their room, breaking stuff, and kicking the walls. The next day he was gone. The story that circulated the next day on the cruise ship was that he had had a complete breakdown. He had been on the ships for something like nine months straight. These types of episodes do happen. Fortunately, they are not often.

Ninety percent of cruise ship crew members are level-headed. They love and enjoy their job on the ship. Like Star Man said, "If you can't have fun on a cruise ship, then you might as well give up." It's easy to say that, but after six months on a ship it is often difficult to not let the monotony, cramped quarters, air quality, food, roommates, the waiting, the petty rules, the crap laundry room, and the red alert days get to you. It can get tough.

Sea days can get to you too. Sea days occur when the ship doesn't dock at a port. These are the days in transit to the next destination. These are the days when the ship is only sailing out at sea. At first, I found the sea days nice and relaxing, and then I quickly began to dread them. Sometimes, like if you are on a ship that is sailing from California to Hawaii and back, you can have more than four sea days in a row. This will give you ship fever.

In fact, sea days are similar to the "rock fever"

phenomenon that occurs with people who live in Hawaii and on other small islands. I lived in Hawaii for a summer, and I was astonished to meet so many native Hawaiians who were simply dying to get off "the rock." The rock is what native Hawaiians call the island of Hawaii, and these locals had developed island fever. This occurs when you hit the wall and can no longer cope with being isolated out in the middle of the ocean any longer. It is like cabin fever, but worse. With cabin fever at least you can, say, get up and walk out of your house and do something else. When you have rock fever, you can't just get up and leave. There is nowhere to go. There is nothing but ocean that stretches to the horizon in every direction. The isolation can feel overwhelming. The desire to be anywhere but on that island can consume you and haunt your dreams.

It's bizarre to think that even in a place as beautiful as Hawaii, people will have this type of obsession come over them where all they want to do is get the hell off that island. Island fever seems to really hit hard after you've explored the entire island; after you know everything that there is to do and after you have visited all the places to see. You feel like there is nothing left to discover. When you live within the continental United States you can always start up your car and just drive down seemingly endless miles of lonely highways. You can drive through deserts, mountains, past beach after beach, and then up into Canada, or down into Mexico. You can easily spend a lifetime just exploring the canyons of Utah. But, on a little island, after just a few months, you've probably seen most of what there is to see.

The ship is just like this. It can be a very fun place to live and work, but after a while you begin to feel trapped. You begin to develop ship fever, and the only cure is to get off the ship. You may be able to diminish the ship fever for a while by getting off the ship and exploring a port, but this is only temporary. The minute you get back onboard, the ship fever returns. You really can't ever leave a ship until your contract is over, so in a way you really are trapped. If you live in Hawaii, although a plane ticket may be expensive, you can leave if you really have the desire to escape.

The only thing worse than sea days are consecutive sea days. They can really get to you. The ship fever will just grow and grow until the ship finally reaches a port somewhere and you find yourself running down the gangway, practically foaming at the mouth, ready to leave that smelly hunk of metal in the dust for a while. Ship fever is no fun, and I can't imagine how intense it must be for crew members who are only able to get off the ship once a week. That is a ship fever I truly never want to experience, and my hat goes off to all the crew members who are able to work in those conditions and still keep a smile on their face day after day. It's amazing.

Interestingly, the main reason ship fever occurs at all is because most crew members are required to work out at sea for such long periods of time. In my opinion, these long contracts really don't make much sense. I don't believe that requiring crew members to work such long contracts serves the crew members or the cruise companies well. From what I have observed, about three months is the perfect length of time for a contract. After three months, most crew members have grown tired of being on the ship and could really use a break for a while. However, in an effort to save money it seems most cruise companies often require crew members to be out at sea for no less than six months. Many crew members' contracts are eight months or longer. I worked one eight-month-long contract and at the end of it, I didn't even want to see a ship for at least a full year. There are a lot of tired, exhausted, and downright miserable crew members out at sea right now as you read this. They aren't enjoying their jobs anymore. They aren't able to offer that high level of customer service that cruise companies really want. All the crew members want is a break. Give them a month off and most crew members will gladly return to the ship, refreshed, rejuvenated, and ready for their next adventure at sea. But in an effort to save a little cash, the cruise industry is effectively shooting itself in the foot. I wholeheartedly believe that crew members would be much happier and much more productive if the cruise companies began offering crew members contracts that were three months long or less. The result would probably be that cruise companies would have a much higher retention rate among the crew, and they would also benefit from having to pay for less training. As a result, the cruise companies would have more return customers because the passengers would be receiving better customer service. Offering shorter contracts could positively change the lives of so many people.

However, worse than ship fever are all the wrecks, fires, and other disasters that can occur on a cruise ship. At the time I was writing this book, the most recent of these disasters involved the *Costa Concordia*. On January 13, 2012, the captain of the *Costa Concordia* apparently guided the cruise ship too close to a rocky Italian shore. There are conflicting reports about the event, but it has been reported that the captain was navigating this close to the coast so that a crew member could wave goodbye to his friends or family on shore. Whatever the reason, the captain ended up sailing the cruise ship directly into a rock and ripping a 160-foot gash into the port side of the hull. The incident occurred in the Tyrrhenian Sea which is about sixty-two miles northwest of Rome. The ship was carrying around 3,000 passengers and 1,000 crew members were on board. Shortly after the ship struck the rock, the engine room was flooded and all the power on the ship was lost. Inside of the ship, passengers and crew members fought their way through flooded and nearly pitch black corridors. The ship drifted towards the coast, eventually listing onto one side just 300 meters from Giglio Island.

Many news outlets also reported that the captain waited more than an hour before ordering an abandon ship. The evacuation of the *Costa Concordia* took more than six hours to complete. Maritime law states that an evacuation should take less than thirty minutes after an abandon ship order is given by the captain of a vessel.

At the time this was originally published, thirty-one people were confirmed dead as a result of the accident, and sixty-four were injured.

Just one month later after the *Costa Concordia* incident, a fire broke out in the engine room aboard the *Costa Allegra*. Costa has clearly had a rough couple of months. The ship completely lost power and was left to drift helplessly in pirate-infested waters off the coast of Tanzania. Then just days later, the *Silver Shadow* operated by Silver Sea Cruise Lines was sailing in heavy fog and accidentally rammed into a cargo ship off the coast of Vietnam. There are all sorts of other unfortunate fates that can occur on cruise ships from fires, muggings while in ports, robberies, and piracy, not to mention icebergs.

I even have my own examples, although I admit they are nothing compared with the *Costa Concordia* tragedy. A ship I once worked aboard was docking in New York City. As we approached the dock, I heard a loud thud. Suddenly, the ship came to an alarming stop. I was nearly thrown onto the floor of my crew cabin. I got up and ran to the crew deck to see what happened. I saw helicopters and airplanes circling above the cruise ship. News reporters had their camera men hanging over the edge of the dock to get a shot of where the cruise ship had rammed into the New York City port. There was an obvious crack in the thick cement of the port wall, and a noticeable dent near the front of the ship's hull.

On another contract, I was assigned a crew cabin that happened to be in the very front of the ship. The cabin was right below the water line, so at night when the seas were high, I could distinctly hear the sound of the waves crashing against the hull. The ocean was just on the other side of the metal wall. The waves that crashed against the hull created a noise like the sound of distant thunder. The waves would shake the walls of my cabin and cause the hull to vibrate. It was enough to keep me up at night, and it certainly did. One night, I was relaxing in my cabin with a friend. We had left Nagasaki, Japan, just an hour or so earlier. The seas were calm. There were no sounds of waves crashing against the hull. Suddenly, I heard a sound as if the ship had hit a brick wall. The entire front of the ship shook. It sounded like we had just impaled Shamu. Yet, we just kept sailing. Crew members talked about it the next day. It was a mystery. No one had any information about the sound we had all heard and the apparent collision that we all felt.

Later that year, the ship was placed into dry dock. When a ship goes into dry dock it is completely lifted out of the water so that the hull can be painted, inspected, and repaired if necessary. The hull needed to be repaired all right. There was a massive dent in the front of the ship, and it was located extremely close to where my cabin had been. A friend asked a nearby officer where the huge dent came from. The officer told her that the ship had hit a concrete piling to the Nagasaki Bridge. It wasn't a whale, it was the Nagasaki Bridge, and it could have been a disaster.

The water that crew members drink on the cruise ship is another frighteningly awful thing to experience.

I am sure that we can all agree that the water on a cruise ship needs to be clean and fit for drinking. Everyone on a cruise ship, after all, wants to be safe, and the norovirus must be stopped at nearly any cost. However, the water on a cruise ship is possibly the most sterile and chemically-treated water on the planet. I would not be surprised if scientists discovered that the water on a cruise ship is unsuitable for human consumption. There has to be a better way to keep crew members hydrated. I definitely would not recommend drinking the water on a cruise ship for any prolonged period of time. If you are going to be working on a ship, bring a water purifier with you, or buy bottled water the entire time you are out at sea. And you might as well shave your head the minute you step onto the ship as a crew member, because the ship's water has the same effect as an over-chlorinated pool.

However, having to leave friends behind is one of the most difficult aspects of working on a ship. A contract on a cruise ship only lasts so long, and when you work on a ship, you can forge very deep friendships. When your contract is over, you often must leave all of those friends behind. Then you are assigned to another ship and you must make new friends all over again. Sometimes, the act of constantly making friends and leaving them behind can make you callused. From the minute you meet other crew members, you begin to see them only as someone that you will eventually have to say goodbye to. For this reason, falling in love on a cruise ship is usually like a mini tragedy waiting to happen. Every day, crew members must say goodbye to friends and lovers only because they are being transferred to another ship, or their contract has come to an end. The port is a place where love is found and lost every day, and whether you find it or lose it mostly depends on whether you are coming, or you are going.

Crew members also have to deal with an astonishing lack of personal freedom. A crew member's life is dictated by ship time. When the ship leaves port, you better be there. When it is chow time, show time, boat drill time, back stage meeting time, or corporate training time, you must be there. A crew member can't choose what they are going to eat for breakfast, lunch, dinner, or anything in between. They have to eat what the chef is cooking up that day. There is a great deal of variety in the food for crew members on the ship, but it is a luxury for those on land to have the ability to say, "I want a Starbucks coffee this morning," and then hop in the car and go buy one. Crew members largely lose control of their lives when they join a cruise ship and that can be difficult to deal with. Crew members are mostly at the mercy of the captain, staff captain, cruise director, and music director; sometimes these are not the kind of people you want in control of your life. A crew member can't choose where they are going. They go where the ship goes. They work when the ship schedule says it is time to work. They play the music that the music director tells them to play, and they do it all until their contracts are over. No one likes to be a subordinate; it can really take the wind out of your sails.

However, there is one thing on the ship that is worse than everything I have mentioned here. It trumps them all. It is Jell-O Pumpkin Pie. I'm serious. I mean, leave it to the cruise ship to take something so perfect and so tasty as pumpkin pie, and turn it into a tasteless, jiggly blob with the texture of a jellyfish. Just looking at a slice of pumpkin pie that is served on a cruise ship leaves you with absolutely zero desire to put it into your mouth. Every time the cruise ship serves this poor excuse for pumpkin pie, there are hundreds of pilgrims and Indians rolling over in their graves. It should be illegal to serve an American treasure such as pumpkin pie in this ridiculous form. It is a travesty, I tell you. Nonetheless, it is a perfectly visible and easily jiggled reflection of what the cruise ship does best. The cruise ship is the ultimate example of how it is entirely possible to turn something with infinite possibility for greatness, something with so much incredible potential, into a mediocre experience at best. They manage it on so many levels from the crew laundry room, to red alert noodles, to poor staff captain choices, and they without a doubt succeed at making the absolute worst pumpkin pie ever. Sometimes, I have those days when I miss the ship, the show band, and the crew parties. I have days when the romantic in me starts swirling with yearnings for my life at sea. But, all I have to do is preheat the oven, cook a real pumpkin pie, and all those desires disappear. At that moment, I will become comfortably disenchanted with the ship once again and immensely grateful for my life on land. However, the feelings of landlubber contentment are not necessarily all caused by the pumpkin pie. They are caused by the fact that I can choose to make the pumpkin pie when I want it. On land, at least I can choose to have pumpkin pie, or choose to have whatever else I want. I can choose to *do* whatever I want, play whatever song with whatever band I want, and choose to make real pumpkin pie that does not look and taste like a washed-up jellyfish.

9

WHAT IS THE BEST PART ABOUT WORKING ON A CRUISE SHIP?

It almost goes without saying, but the travel is hands down the best part about working on a cruise ship. I have been a travel junkie for as long as I can remember. To me the world is just meant to be explored, and the cruise ship gives crew members a first class ride to the most beautiful coastal ports on the planet. And from the port, crew members can definitely explore the rest of these coastal destinations on their own. For someone who is desperately addicted, completely obsessed, and absolutely passionate about traveling and exploring every corner of the planet, there is no better way to spend a misspent youth than working as a cruise ship crew member.

As you sail across ocean after ocean, somehow the world doesn't become a smaller place. On a cruise ship, you travel by sea. You extend the great seafaring tradition that has been a deep and rich part of the human experience since the dawn of man. In doing so, while sailing through the seas, bays, and inlets of the world, you once and for all get a feel for just how massive this planet really is.

On a cruise ship, you get to experience the blue of the earth, and so you get to sail around the largest part of the planet that only a few will ever get the chance to deeply explore. However, you don't just zoom over the oceans in an airplane, or dip a toe into it from the shore. You feel the spray of the ocean when high seas thunder against the hull. You see the dolphins and whales as they breach in the distance and race the mysterious metal beast that has entered into their waters. You stand at the bow of the ship at sunset and sail away from the coast as dolphins playfully jump and lead the way as if they are towing the cruise liner to its next incredible destination. You get to experience how it feels to sail on a ship as it slices through the sea. And as a crew member, you get to watch it all from the bow of the ship—from the best seat in the house.

As crew members, we have the opportunity to travel around the world. We get to deeply experience destinations and people from every corner of the globe. And when you do this, you are able to develop a sense for just how beautiful and special the earth really is. Crew members get to hear the tongue twisting languages, eat the exotic and strange foods, explore mysterious landscapes, and feel the sand of a thousand beaches between their toes.

When I tell people that I have worked on cruise ships, I always get asked the same question, "What is the best place you have ever been?" It is an impossible question because there is no "best." Every place is extremely unique, and every destination holds special memories that I cherish. During the five years I spent working on cruise ships, I mostly sailed in the Caribbean. I must have visited ninety percent of the ports that cruise ships sail to in that part of the world. And when you work on a cruise ship, sometimes you visit the same places hundreds of times. This can certainly become a monotonous nightmare after a while for some locations. For other destinations, this repetitive travel becomes an amazing opportunity to thoroughly explore the place, always searching for a new beach to walk, a quiet waterfall on a river to jump from, a new hotel pool to swim in, or a new restaurant to indulge. Crew members get to search for that special place that really captures the spirit of that location, or at least lets you use the pool for free and has great prices on tacos and beer. Going back to the same place gives crew members the opportunity to dig deep into the culture and to explore the coastal area completely. As a result, crew members usually come out with an incredible knowledge, appreciation, and understanding of the destination.

There also is a genuinely rejuvenating and energizing quality to living on a vessel that is always going somewhere. The ship is always moving and always searching. There is nothing behind a cruise ship but exhaust and a wake. The past is not a place you go to on a cruise ship. The calm waters are always in front of the ship, and the horizon is at once the ending of the landscape and the beginning of possibility. There is always the next port, that next island, that next great adventure to look forward to. The experience is going to be different every time you sail. Even if you have visited an island a million times, if you look for it, you can always find something new and wonderful to experience. The cruise ship is always racing forward. You can feel this forward motion even when you are inside the ship. You can feel the ship racing through the ocean and battling the sea. You can hear the hum of the hull and the pounding of the waves as the ship moves always closer towards that unknown future filled with limitless potential. And the ship moves through this water with unmatched power, determination, and certainty. This feeling gets inside of you—this love of the unknown horizon, this passion for the adventurous future, this obsession with racing forward, this embracing of the ceaseless movement, this enduring dedication to battle towards paradise. It becomes so much a part of you that when the ship stops—when the ship slows and ropes up to the dock, and the creaking and the cracking of the ship quiets, and the hum of the metal hull dies, and everything becomes still and hushed—you are left with an eerily empty feeling.

The ship races onwards around the world. I have been on ships that have sailed throughout the

Caribbean exploring Jamaica, St. Thomas, St. Martin, all sorts of ports in the Bahamas and Mexico, the Cayman Islands, and places like the Turks and Caicos, as well as little private islands owned by the cruise companies with long, pristine, sandy white beaches that belong in dreams and on postcards. I boarded ships sailing up the east coast from New York to Boston, up into Canada to places like Halifax and St. John, and up the west coast all the way from Acapulco to Vancouver. The ship has taken me through Alaska, to Australia, New Zealand, Papua New Guinea, Indonesia, Malaysia, Borneo, China, and Japan. And all of this travel has been because of music. Music was the vehicle that crossed all of those oceans, brought me to all of those ports, and allowed me to experience all of those wonderful places. Being a musician also allowed me to live on a cruise ship in the same hallway with a cast of the most insanely beautiful dancers you can imagine, but that's all I'm going to say about that.

As I have said before, most crew members only get a half day off once a week. However, musicians and the other entertainers are able to get off at almost every port. The passengers are off the ship, so entertainers have this time off as well. Being able to explore every port is one of the greatest aspects of being a musician, an entertainer, or having any other job on a cruise ship where the working hours are determined by the presence of passengers on the ship. The musicians, dancers, singers, and art auctioneers are some of the lucky ones on the ship that get to experience every destination. Now, this can really get under the skin of the other crew members, and I certainly understand why, but for those of us who have this luxury, it is one of the best parts of working on a cruise ship.

Another wonderful aspect of working on a cruise ship is that you never have to drive a car. Imagine a life without traffic. Imagine a life without ever having to step into the driver's seat. Imagine being able to walk to work every day, and being able to go the bar and drink as much as you want and not have to worry about crashing into someone on the way home, getting pulled over and issued a DUI, or having someone else crash into you.

If you work on a cruise ship, and especially if you play in the band, you also have the world's best commute to work. You just wake up and walk fifty feet or so and you're there. There is no sitting and waiting in a blood-pressure rising, bumper-to-bumper wasteland. You never have to drive to get to a restaurant—there are plenty on the ship. You never have to pick up the keys and drive to the movie theater—there is one on the ship. You never have to ride in a plane to get to a tropical paradise—the ship goes there every day. It is wonderful, and it is wonderfully safe too. In the United States, motor vehicle crashes are the leading cause of death for individuals between the ages of five and thirty-four, so what better and safer place to spend your youth than sailing around the world on a cruise ship and never having to step foot in a car the entire time.

Also, sit back, close your eyes, and imagine what life would be like if you never had to worry about money. Imagine not even thinking about money. Now that I am back on land, I often catch myself spending quite a bit of time thinking about money. Imagine never having to worry about whether you are going to make rent because there is no rent. Imagine never having to worry about how much food is going to cost, because on a cruise ship there is food everywhere, and even though sometimes it tastes like ketchup-covered raccoon snouts, it's free. Sometimes it's even filet mignon or chicken fingers. Imagine never having to worry about how much the price of gas is going up. When you work on a cruise ship, you don't have to buy any gas. On a cruise ship, you work on an all-expense-paid vacation to everywhere. Let the party begin, right?

At one point while I worked on the cruise ships, I remember having something like fifty dollars a month in expenses. I had a car back home and my only expense was a minimal amount of car insurance. I canceled my phone plan because we were sailing in an area where I couldn't get reception. No rent. No food. No gas. No mortgage. No gym membership. No medical bills (because the clinic is free for crew members). No car payment. No health insurance. No nothing. Just fifty bucks going out the door every month. I could spend everything I made on the ship on whatever I wanted. I could blow it in the ports on tacos and coronas with limes, or renting jeeps and exploring islands, or on one dollar Stella Artois in the crew bar, or on more and more drum gear when I got back home. And that is exactly what I did. It was great.

On the cruise ship you never have to cook. Imagine

not having to cook a single meal for eight months straight because there is a chef who is paid to cook as much lentil curry as you want. On a cruise ship, you never have to do the dishes, take out the trash, clean your room, clean your own bathroom, or make your bed. Ahhhh, that was a dream come true not ever having to make my bed. You don't have to do any of this, because when you get on board you are assigned a steward who will do all of it for you for about one dollar a day. It is incredible. It is a dream. It leaves you with so much time, so little stress, and such a tiny amount of responsibility.

I compare working on the cruise ship with hiking the Appalachian Trail, minus the clean air and sunshine. On the Appalachian Trail, your life becomes this singly focused goal of walking the trail. All you have to do is wake up and walk. On a cruise ship, all you really have to do is wake up and work. For a musician, all you have to do is wake up and play music for three to five hours a day. It makes life really simple. You don't have to do anything else but play music and have fun, of course. All the responsibility of living life on land is gone. All the hustling disappears. Someone in the show band said to me once, "A cruise ship is the ultimate test of a person's will. On a cruise ship, you can be as constructive or as destructive as you want." And this is absolutely true. You can spend your time drinking, eating, and sleeping, or you can spend your time on the cruise ship honing your skills on your instrument, getting off the ship and really experiencing the world. The decision is completely up to the crew member.

However, crew members often end up spending all of their free time in the crew bar. There is no denying that on a cruise ship, the crew likes to party. There is always some type of party happening on the ship. The crew bar is where most of the action happens, and if you are ever on a cruise as a passenger and can make it happen, I suggest you try to find a way to get down to the crew bar and see it yourself. This is where the crew goes to drink, dance, and de-stress, of course. There is a crowd nearly every night in the crew bar, and once a month or so the cruise ship company pays for an official crew party. There is usually a theme to the night like "70's Disco Party" or "Dress up Like a Superhero." Once in a while, there is a "Band Night" and the show band will set up in the crew bar and play for the crew for a few hours. Then there are the deck parties. An open deck is roped off and the entire crew has the opportunity to gather out under the stars as the ship sails through the night, and the crew dances to that odd mix of international dance music that is only played by cruise ship DJs.

However, the greatest parties of all are the cabin parties. If the party in the crew bar is going strong, it often continues back to someone's crew cabin, and preferably to a large cabin with porthole windows— so in other words, someone with officer status. Once in a while, you are lucky enough to find yourself at a party hosted by a cruise director or someone else high up on the food chain. You are lucky because the cruise directors don't just have one room, they have two.

Most cruise directors have a living room with a couch, a few plushy arm chairs, a small wet bar off to one side, a big flat-screen TV, and either a nice big window that frames the ocean as it glides by, or a series of brass fitted porthole windows lining the wall. Cruise directors also have a separate bedroom in their cabin with a big, comfy, full-size bed. Cruise directors never have a hard time finding a girlfriend when they have luxurious rooms like this on the ship. For a crew member, stepping into a cruise director's room either makes you want to quit (because you realize how deprived you are), or makes you want to try harder to become the cruise director's best friend. Either way, envy plays a large role in the experience.

While parties hosted by the cruise director do happen, most of the time crew members party in a crew cabin where the peasants live down below the water line. And the cabin party is a freak of necessity. Crew members get to the point where they have seen everything on the ship. They have been to the disco a million times. They have walked down the same promenade for months. They have grown sick of the crew bar, and they refuse to spend another minute in the stench of the crew mess. Crew members get to the point where the last thing they want to do is walk around in a passenger area. They reach a point where they avoid passengers at all costs. I mean, who wants to be enjoying a night off hanging out in the disco with your name tag on and have a passenger that closely resembles the size of a beached whale walk up and ask you to go get him a Sprite. Somehow, this can zap the fun right out of your night off. In fact, crew members actually grow so tired of passengers that they start to treat the passenger areas as veritable war zones. The crew area is the only green zone on the ship. And crew cabins are the real safe zones where crew members can finally take off the name tag, remove the clip-on bow tie, stop constantly shaving their faces, clean the gel out their hair, kick back, have some fun, and hang out with the rest of the crew. At a cabin party, you'll find twelve or twenty other completely exhausted crew members that want to loosen their ties as well.

Crew members are all a part of the same club. Becoming a crew member is like joining a fraternity or a sorority. Crew members are all experiencing the same and oftentimes monotonous reality of ship life. Crew members are all racing through the same ocean, towards the same islands. They all experience the same cabin parties where they hang onto bed rails and desks in the crew cabins to keep from falling over as the ship breaks through the waves of the sea. And when crew members loosen their ties, most of them drink like pirates minus the guns, parrots, eye patches, and wooden legs... and well, any semblance of sailing skills. Most crew members wouldn't know a jib from a mast, but they definitely know the difference between a single and a double malt whiskey. The cabin parties are an institution on cruise ships. They are where the true camaraderie and morale that absolutely buoy the ship is formed, and where that crew is kept happy, relaxed, and unified. Crew parties are the best parties on the seven seas.

Living a life aboard a cruise ship is an eternal summer. A cruise ship always goes where it's warm and sails to islands at the most beautiful time to visit. A cruise ship is not sailing to a destination when that port is experiencing a rainy season, peak mosquito season, mud season, snow blizzard season, or sand storm season. The cruise ship company isn't going to pass out rain slicks, mud shoes, goggles, and down jackets. The cruise ship simply isn't going to these destinations. If you're going to Alaska or Canada, it will be summer. If you're sailing down to the hottest islands in the Caribbean, you can bet that you're going during the dead of the American winter. The cruise ship stays on an endless bearing with fall straight ahead and winter far behind; always nestling into that little, perfect, warm, dry, cozy, sweet spot where crew members can always get a tan. The cruise ship always sails right where you want to go, right when you want to go there, and this is a great way to live.

The cruise ship also avoids any and all situations that could possibly be unpleasant for passengers. If a hurricane is whipping up off the coast of Africa and is hurling towards a cruise ship's itinerary, the ship doesn't turn around and cower inside the port of Miami. The cruise ship alters its bearing, skirts around the edge of the swirling hurricane, and sails off to a different beautiful island where the palms trees aren't getting ripped from the ground. If a war, a drought, or a tsunami happens somewhere in the world, the cruise ship just doesn't sail to that port until the violence or tragedy subsides. The cruise ship only sails towards the sun-kissed and smiling faces of the world and leaves the tragedy of disasters and conflicts in the wake.

Ship life and the cruising experience may not be reality, but it is definitely relaxing. Ship life is the ultimate vacation from stress. If the world were a giant lemon meringue pie, you may not get the entire pie, but you definitely get the largest and sweetest slice when you're living on a cruise ship. Who wants to eat a whole lemon meringue pie anyway? Sometimes, if you eat the whole thing, it just makes you sick. I think the crackerjack marketing department at Princess Cruise Lines said it best with their slogan "Escape Completely." If you want to escape, then go on a cruise. If you want to escape completely, try living on a cruise ship for six months. I escaped so effectively during a six month contract that when I arrived back on land, I couldn't even remember how to make a cup of coffee for myself, and my blood type is coffee.

Having the opportunity to work on a cruise ship offers crew members experiences that they otherwise would not have been able to afford. Passengers are able to come on cruise ships and experience all of the adventures in ports around the world because they could afford to spend the money to buy a ticket on a cruise ship (and cruises are damn expensive). I would venture to say that 90 percent of crew members would not be able to afford a ticket on a cruise ship. If it were not for the opportunity to work on these ships, most crew members would never have the opportunity to walk through ancient Mayan temples on the Mexican coast, or body surf in the glassy and curling waves at

Bondi Beach in Sydney, or sip a *mai tai* in Hawaii. And crew members get to do all of these things for free. One hundred percent free. I sat down and calculated exactly how much free cruising I have received. Over the five years that I worked on cruise ships, when I take out about twelve months for the breaks that I took, I spent a solid four years cruising around the world. There are fifty-two weeks in a year. This means I spent 208 weeks on a cruise ship. A good deal on a weeklong cruise is $500. So, during the five years I worked on cruise ships, I took $104,000 worth of cruises. As if this isn't enough, I was paid an average of $2,400 a month (a total of $86,400) to take these cruises, and I also had a blast playing music while I was on them. Not bad, eh?

I truly love to see so many people from around the world having the opportunity to explore their world by working on these cruise ships. Cruise ships help break down the barriers of cultures and the borders that divide us. A cruise ship allows people to go and explore *our* world. This is the way it should be. After all, the world does belong to *all* of us, doesn't it? I can't speak for anyone else, but I know that I would not have seen and experienced so much, and traveled so far, if I had not stepped foot onto a cruise ship. I loved being part of a crew that is comprised of people from all over the world, and to sail aboard a cruise ship as it raced through the seas and explored all of the vastly different countries that the crew members come from.

The fact that the crew does come from all over the world is one of the best parts about working on a ship. How many people are able to sit and talk about their life experiences at a table comprised of people from India, Russia, Indonesia, England, Romania, and America? One of my favorite things about the cruise ship was being able to sit down on a sea day and drink coffee with a crew member from a different country, and get them talking about what it was like to grow up in the country where they live. You discover very quickly that the cold war was very different for the Russians, and if you lend your ear and ask the right questions, you will receive firsthand accounts of conflicts and world-shaping moments in modern history that happened across the globe. It is one thing to watch a news story in 1992 that reported on the Serbian-Croatian conflict, and an entirely different experience to board a cruise ship in 2008 and receive a riveting firsthand account from someone who lived through the wars. I cherished the eye-opening opportunity to deeply understand how different everyday life is for people all over the globe. It somehow gave me a stronger sense of who I am, and how unique my own experiences are, and how much of my fate and experience was determined by the fact that I happened to be born in a particular place on a particular day.

Ship life gives a crew member the opportunity to step outside their own lives, step outside the influences of their culture, their family culture, and their friends. When a crew member joins a ship, their "real life" stops for minute, and they can look back at their life with a new perspective from the sea. Crew members can see themselves from afar. Ship life allowed me to take a much needed vacation from my own reality, and on the cruise ship I realized that my own reality was far from being the only reality that exists. The cruise ship changed me in this way, and in ship life I was given the opportunity to reinvent myself every time I stepped onto a new ship. I would take with me what I had learned from the last little floating city I lived on, and then carefully apply those lessons to the next. Shape-shifters are not just something from the pages of a science-fiction paperback; you see one every time you see a cruise ship crew member. Crew members often are shaped by the cruise ship into something more aware and much more beautiful than what they were the first time they walked up that gangway and stepped foot onto a cruise ship.

For a musician, the cruise ship allows you to focus on your music. In fact, the cruise ship is one of the last remaining gigs in the world where a musician can still be in the minor leagues of music and make a good living only performing. On a cruise ship, musicians don't have to waste their time working as a waiter or on a construction site somewhere just to pay the bills. Besides those brilliantly fun boat drills, all a cruise ship musician must do is play music. I am forever grateful to the cruise companies that I worked for that gave me the opportunity to do nothing but focus on my instrument, hone my skills, and play music with other phenomenally talented musicians. These days, only having to work as a musician is a real luxury, and I am thankful that this luxury lives on aboard cruise ships all around the world.

As difficult as ship life can be, every crew member begins to miss it after they leave the ship. There is nothing like the feeling I got when I stepped onto a new ship after a few months of vacation time. After the initial culture shock and the adjustment to the awesome smell of drying paint, I would find a quiet spot on the crew deck as the ship sailed out of port for the first time. I would feel the wind divert past my gelled hair and burn against my close-shaven face. I would look down at my name tag, and as the ship began to sail forward, a familiar feeling would sink in. I would feel the freedom of a life without rent, insurance, gas, and food costs. I would feel the wind deliver a life where I would never have to clean another dish, make my own bed, cook my own meals, or clean my own filthy bathroom again.

You start to feel excited as the ship thrusts forward towards a horizon that leads to beach after sunny beach after topless beach. You put aside the concerns about your neurotic and freakishly tidy roommate that you are convinced has been put on this earth with the sole purpose of crowding and annoying you. Then you take a deep breath of fairly clean air that is slightly mixed with the exhaust of the cruise ship, you nibble on a chicken finger, wash it down with a Stella Artois, and realize that you are feeling the pleasures of a life at sea. You realize that what you are feeling is what brought you back to ship life.

You exhale. And with that breath and the sinking of your shoulders, you relax into your new life that is free from mindless chores and where money is of no concern. The ship races forward and charges through the sea, towards an endless summer and on a bearing to some sunny, palm-tree-lined paradise. You relax and realize that you have returned to the ship life that you love. You realize that you are finally back on cruise control, and that cruise control is the only way you ever want to live.

10

WHY WOULD ANYONE EVER STOP WORKING ON A CRUISE SHIP?

The answer to this is simple. It was a Monday. It was the fourth sea day in a row. The ship was on red alert. Way more than 2 percent of the ship had contracted the norovirus. I was searching for a horse tranquilizer, and I had already decided which friends would be the best crew members to take with me when I escaped on a lifeboat at midnight. I had spent the last week watching the perfect cruise derail from the norovirus. On the first day of the cruise, a few thousand people climbed aboard the cruise ship. They were all smiling, excited, and looking forward to cruising Alaska's inside passage. They were confident that they would get to see whales, or harness and ride a bald eagle over the snow-capped mountains or something. Then the norovirus showed up to the party. I watched these same goofy-smiling passengers devolve into miserable people stumbling through the hallways and drooling with sickness as they scuttled towards the medical center.

In the crew mess there was nothing to eat but steamy noodles with olive oil and a clear, plastic bin full of bread rolls. Just to top it all off, lurking somewhere on the dessert buffet was an especially bland and gelatinous slice of pumpkin pie made from jellyfish guts. Crew members were bracing for the horses and pillories to come back out. The crew was officially banned from passenger areas. This was Captain's orders. Crew members were trapped in the stuffy and cramped crew area where we all could breathe the same virus infused air. No one on board could wait for the ship to reach Seattle. Compared to this, even a rainy day in Seattle spent in a crowded booth at Starbucks sounded like a trip to Disneyworld.

As if this wasn't enough, the hot tub on the crew deck had been closed the entire time I had been aboard the cruise ship. As I said before, if there is ever a time that you want to grab a cappuccino in a thin paper cup from the crew mess and sit in a bubbling hot tub set to 105 degrees with a cast full of dancers, it is when you are cruising through Alaska's inside passage watching snow-capped mountains pass by while the cruise ship dodges whales. Every day, I would walk out onto the deck with a towel in one hand, a cappuccino in the other, and swimming trunks on. I would be praying that I would find a hot tub that was steaming, bubbling, and full of dancers. Yet, I never did. Every day, I would just have to sit on the hot tub steps, sip my coffee, and wonder what moron decided to close the hot tub at a time like this.

These are the times when you are ready to pack it up, head home, and never see a cruise ship again as long as you live. Every crew member gets tired of the monotony, the noise, the petty rules, the smell, the smoke, and the food. I was tired of all these things too at this point. However, this time was different. This time I knew without a doubt that it was time to pack my bags and walk away from ship life. I had suffered through four sea days in a row, the ship was on red alert, and everyone around me was sick with norovirus. There was nothing to eat but noodles and bread rolls. The hot tub was closed. I absolutely had to get off the cruise ship, and this time I wanted to be off the ship forever. I didn't really have a choice in the matter. I knew that it was either turn in my name badge or go completely mad.

I was starving, and so I walked to the crew mess for some more noodles and jellyfish pie. The crew mess was completely sterilized from floor to ceiling. I was surprised to see that the cruise company didn't have some of the smaller and extremely lightweight crew members who worked in the housekeeping department using suction-cup shoes so they could scrub down the ceiling. The room smelled like a bleach factory. At nearly every entrance, there was someone making sure that every crew member washed their hands. I had to wash my hands when I walked in the door. Then I washed my hands before I went up to the buffet, and washed my hands before I poured a drink. I had to wash my hands for just looking at the guy telling everyone to wash their hands. At times like this, the crew is really on edge. Every crew member is pretty much required to work even longer hours than normal to ensure that the passenger areas are constantly and thoroughly cleaned. Combine long working hours with the fact that crew members can't leave the crew area, and you end up with a ship full of rather exhausted, stressed, and exceptionally edgy sailors.

After washing my hands like five times in a row, I finally made it to the bread roll bin. That's when I noticed something unnerving. Crew members were coming into the crew mess from a small side door. This small entrance effectively bypassed all of the hand washing police. None of the crew members that came into the crew mess from this entrance were washing their hands. I watched a crew member walk right through the side door, wipe his nose with the front of his hand, grab the bread roll tongs, and serve himself up a couple of the daily specials. There was no way that I was willingly going to expose myself to the norovirus. I hadn't located any horse tranquilizers yet, and a lifeboat escape may be too dangerous. We were sailing in cold Alaskan waters. I imagined my rogue crew of mutineers kidnapping a social host, stealing the champagne, and then in a drunken stupor capsizing the lifeboat. An escape was out of the question. I had to suck it up and stay on the ship. However, there was no way that I was going to get norovirus, so there was no way I was going to touch those grimy tongs in the bread roll bin.

I left the tongs alone, and simply grabbed a few bread rolls out of the bin with my hands, making sure I didn't touch any of the other bread rolls in there. I placed the rolls onto my plate. Suddenly, an Indian security guard with a mustache like a cheap extra from the set of *Three's Company* materialized out of thin air as if he was instantly generated from the spool of a Bollywood B-movie.

"Did jou jus take a bread roll with your hands?" he asked. His head moved rapidly from side to side as if it was very loosely attached to his neck as he accused me of first-degree bread roll touching.

"Well, there is this door here that people are...," I said. The security guard cut me off before I could even begin to explain how I became involved in "Roll-Gate."

"Did jou or did jou not just touch these bread rolls? Do you not know that we are under red alert? Do you understand that you are supposed to be using these tongs?"

"Well, look, those tongs are disgusting, and I am trying to keep myself from getting sick, and..."

"So you don't think you have to follow de rules dat everyone else has to follow?" he said.

I wanted to bring up the issues I had regarding other crew members who choose to not respect lines or wear deodorant.

"Everyone has to use these tongs," the Indian

version of Tom Selleck continued. "We are all responsible for all other crew members on this ship when we are under red alert. There are very strict rules that we must follow, and you are breaking these rules and could cause everyone else to get sick." With that he just turned around and stormed off.

Later that night after my performance in the main theater was over, I was called into the cruise director's office. The cruise director threatened to fire me for the bread roll scandal. After a great deal of debating, the cruise director decided to give me a written warning. I was thirty years old, and I was getting written up for touching a bread roll. It felt like high school again. It was ridiculous, but this is how ridiculous ship life can be. And this time I had reached my true breaking point. My contract on the cruise ship would be ending in just a few days, and I decided that it would be a long time before I would voluntarily set foot on a cruise ship as a crew member again. I needed a vacation from the largest sailing vacation in the world. I needed one more trip to the midnight buffet and one more good party in the crew bar, and then I would be ready to hang it up and never look back.

I had also reached an impasse as a musician as well. I felt that the music I was performing was limiting. The music was not limited by the degree of challenge, variety, musicianship, or the passion that I had for the music we were playing. However, the music had limited potential. On land, a musician has a much greater potential to find financial success and reach a considerably larger audience. However, on a ship you are working for the ship. Your job is to entertain and provide music for the passengers, and that is as far as the music you make will ever go. Besides, I hadn't received a pay raise in two years. I felt like I was spinning my wheels.

These limitations can often zap the passion right out of a musician, and it can be a real drag to perform with passionless musicians who are only working on the ship for a paycheck. Now don't get me wrong, there are plenty of musicians on the ships that haven't allowed themselves get to this point. There are plenty of musicians on cruise ships that keep their passion buoyed with their deep love for music. There are plenty of guys out on the ships that make the job incredible and keep the band cooking. Yet, I saw myself losing my passion for the music that I was performing on the ship. This was frightening. If I wanted to preserve my passion for music, I had to leave the cruise ship.

There was something else that drove me from the ship as well. I wanted my freedom back. This drives more crew members away from the ship than the turkey ball soups and the red alert cruises. I had to leave the ship if I wanted to regain my freedom and reclaim my independence. I was tired of being on ship time. I wanted to be on my own watch. I was living a life where someone else controlled my schedule. I knew it was time to grab the rudder myself, take control of the helm, and start steering my own ship.

I finally reached the end of my long contract, and I took that last walk down the rickety gangway. I turned around to look at the ship one last time. The cruise ship had been my home for the last six months. I smiled when I realized that I wouldn't have to be back aboard the ship in six or seven hours, and I wouldn't have to eat another bowl of lentil curry for at least a few months. For a crew member, it is a great feeling to know that you are leaving red alert, boat drills, and your tiny, sardine-can-sized cabin behind for a while. So, after all the long and hard goodbyes with all of the great friends you made on your contract, you run down that gangway as fast as you can. You walk out into the port, and you catch a taxi to the airport where you will board a plane that will take you home and back to a life that you control—a plane that only flies a one-way route to freedom.

You arrive home, run to your room, climb in bed, and turn off all the lights. You pull the covers over you, and then you celebrate for a moment the gargantuan size of your bed which has suddenly become an exceptionally novel thing. After making snow angels under the covers, and thoroughly stretching out in every possible direction to take full advantage of the bed's incredible width, you close your eyes.

What you realize is that the world outside of a cruise ship, the world above the water line, is chillingly quiet. It is unnervingly quiet. The world is still, and with this stillness creeps a feeling of stagnation. Without the hum of the hull as the ocean roars past the sides of the ship, and without the creaking of the walls, floor, and ceiling as the cruise ship battles over waves and fights against the ceaseless watery fists of the sea—

there is only silence in the world. The world becomes still and motionless. The sea rocked you to sleep for months, and now that you are out of its arms, you feel lost somehow. You feel strange without these sounds and without these familiar motions of a ship. There is no ocean splashing and spraying outside of the bedroom anymore, and there is light everywhere. The streetlights, the headlights of cars, and the dim lights from nearby rooms seep through the crack at the bottom of the door. All of them seem like jail-break spotlights shining into your room. On the ship, there is no light in the room at night. When you walk into your crew cabin and turn off the lights, you are left with the most absolute and complete darkness. You are nestled below the ocean and tucked into a room with no windows.

So, you lay there in bed and realize that you will have to make that bed when you wake up. You will have to cook your breakfast, clean your dishes, and somehow you will have to find a way to fall asleep in all of this light, in the stark stillness of this motionless world. And you find this very difficult to do. Days later, you find yourself thinking about money—something you haven't done in months. You run out of groceries, and so you have to go to the grocery store, and you have to drive a car to get to the grocery store. You haven't driven in months. You haven't been in traffic in years. When you get to the grocery store, you can't believe how much they are asking for filet mignon, oranges, kiwis, or real pumpkin pie. You used to eat mounds of this stuff for free. All of this becomes very stressful. For a crew member, the transition from ship life back to a life on land can take months. Sometimes, the difficulty of the transition is enough to drive you back to the ship. It is enough to send you running back up the gangway and back to the ship life that you know so well and love so much. You want to return to the familiar and back to a life where you will be able to sleep in the arms of the sea and won't have to make your bed when you wake up.

However, no matter how much time passes, the sea and your life as a cruise ship crew member will always be a part of you. You can never leave it completely behind. There always will be a little more salt in your blood, and probably a lot more rum. Once you work on a cruise ship, you will always be a crew member. You will always belong to that group of people forever scattered around the world that know what you're talking about when you say "red alert" and double over in exaggerated pain and anguish. They will always know what you mean when you smile about a cabin party, or gag at the thought of another plate of lentil curry in the crew mess. They have been there just like you. They have fought the Filipino Mafia in the crew laundry room. They have lived in a windowless sardine can just like you. They have battled through the sea, night after rocky night, and looked up at the same brightly shining stars into a pitch-black Caribbean sky from the edge of the crew deck. They have surely eaten a slice of that tasty pumpkin pie.

They know what it's like to live a life of adventure on the sea and the difficulty of leaving it behind. They know what it is like to travel the world, see thousands of miles of the planet's coastline, live a life in an endless summer, and live on an island that is always moving from one paradise to the next. They know what it means to live on cruise control. They know what it is really like to be a cruise ship crew member. After it is all over, the memories of ship life still carry on within you. No matter how much time passes and no matter where you are in the world, you will never be able to hear the deep and thundering sound of a ship's horn the same way again. Because when the ship's horn blows and echoes across the sea, you will be filled with the often fond and sometimes nauseating memories of your life as a cruise ship crew member. The sound of that ship's horn will leave you with a feeling like the first time you saw a clown at a friend's birthday party as a child. You will feel completely uncertain whether you should run towards it, or run away as fast as your little legs can run.

The following is an excerpt from:

THE CRUISE SHIP CAPERS

AN ART HEIST ON THE HIGH SEAS

A fiction book by Joshua Kinser

Now available at Amazon.com as an eBook and in print.

1

DAY 2. NASSAU. OCTOBER 4. 1:55 PM.

Bianchi Valentini is late to everything, even to one of the biggest art heists in cruise ship history. Daniel rubs his ear lobe. It appears casual, but he's adjusting the earpiece that allows him to communicate with the rest of his group. Months of preparation are behind the gang of four that he's assembled, and everything is going as planned.

They purchased their tickets individually for the seven-day Caribbean cruise aboard the *Star of the Seas*, and they intentionally showed up late to the Port of Miami. The ship sailed without them, and so they had no choice but to fly to the Bahamas on a puddle-jumper, and then catch the ship in Nassau. But it was all part of the plan.

Once the plane landed, Daniel gave instructions. The group will clear customs in Nassau, and then immediately disband. They will regroup at the gangway five minutes before the ship's horn blows and signals the final all aboard. The embarkation must be rushed. This is vital.

Now Daniel waits for the rest of his group to reassemble. He's standing between two cruise ships at the end of the long concrete pier, dwarfed by the massive hulls that soar above him. He feels like he's standing inside of a steep canyon with walls made of white metal instead of rock. Waves slap against the bow of the ship. A heavy wind blows in from the east.

It's early October and tropical storm *Igor* is ripping thatched roofs off rum bars and unraveling cigars in Cuba. The Captain of the *Star of the Seas*, Christopher Casteel, has informed the two security guards at the gangway that he doesn't care about the three late passengers. Captain Casteel has bigger problems. He needs to leave on time in order to skirt the edge of the storm. If the passengers don't show in the next five minutes, the security guards will pull in the gangway. They will sail to Grand Turk three passengers short.

Daniel stands fifty feet from the gangway. He can hear the metal gangway scraping against the concrete pier. He turns toward the ocean. His close-cropped hair compliments the sharp features of his face—a large Romanesque nose and chiseled cheek bones. He watches as white caps dissolve into the turquoise sea, a perfect mixture of beauty and turmoil.

"Have you seen her?" Daniel says.

"No," a voice answers from his earpiece. "I'm watching, and we might have a problem. The Captain ordered the gangway closed in five minutes. Maybe we should move without her." Bartek is standing on the pier near the back of the cruise ship. Two olive-green duffle bags sit at his feet. He's wearing an earpiece like Daniel's, khaki pants, black wraparound shades, and a hibiscus patterned tropical shirt that's flapping in the wind. His twin brother Patryk should arrive right behind Bianchi. Daniel recruited the Polish twins because they are brilliant and, well, because they are twins. Bartek has twice the brains of Patryk, he's a gadget type of guy, can build a computer out of a box of paperclips and a bag of Funyuns.

"She'll be here," Daniel says.

"Let's hope so."

"You know, I was reading my Bible last night—"

"You're a strange guy you know that?" Bartek says.

"I flipped it open, just to see what page it would land on. It turned to the Book of Luke, chapter 12, verse 19. You know what that verse says?"

"That we're all about to be filthy rich."

"It said: 'And I'll say to myself, Take life easy; eat, drink and be merry. But God said to him, You fool! This very night your life will be demanded from you.' We need to stay on our toes. There's something more to this one. Something deeper. I feel it. I just—"

"Here she is," Bartek says. "She's about a hundred yards from the gangway. Patryk's about 30 feet behind her."

"Wait for my word," Daniel says. "This must be fluid. It must be perfect."

Daniel walks toward the ship, pulling a black suitcase behind him. Before he sees Bianchi he hears the clicking of her high-heels echoing off the cruise ship's metal hull. Daniel asked her to dress sexy. He looks at Bianchi and realizes that she's a woman who knows what sexy really means.

She's wearing hot-pink heels, a skintight turquoise miniskirt, and a palm-tree print tank top that's more cleavage than fabric. It's obvious that she's spent a great deal of time in Paris because she understands that the right outfit can be a serious act of foreplay.

"We're ready for you, girl," Daniel says.

"Is this sexy enough?" Bianchi says.

"You're a goddess, baby," Daniel says. "Everyone. Wait for my word. I'm your eyes now."

"I'm ready," Patryk says. He's wearing the same outfit as his brother—tropical shirt, black shades, khaki pants, but no duffel bags.

Bianchi walks up the gangway first. The security guard's eyes go straight to her cleavage. To Bianchi's left is the conveyor belt that pushes luggage through an x-ray machine. To her right is the check-in kiosk, a small podium with a slot in the front where passengers slide in their ID cards.

One of the security guards is standing behind the x-ray machine. His nametag reads, TAPAN CHOPRA, SECURITY, INDIA. He has a thick Tom-Selleck style mustache, a pudgy face, and an overenthusiastic smile that's clearly insincere. The other guard is behind the kiosk. He's rail thin and clean shaven. His name tag reads, VIJAY PATEL, SECURITY, INDIA.

They're both wearing light-blue security guard uniforms that look more like cheap Halloween costumes than something official. They both also have dark bags under their eyes, bags earned from six months of fourteen-hour shifts, chain smoking, and a severe vitamin deficiency that is the result of eating nothing but the food in the crew mess. Unfortunately, this is the inevitable aesthetic destination of most cruise ship crewmembers.

Bartek is behind Bianchi, and he starts walking up the gangway. Daniel waits at the bottom of the gangway. Patryk stays about twenty feet behind Daniel, out of sight of the security guards.

"Left side," Daniel says quietly. Bianchi moves toward the x-ray machine and places an enormous bag onto the conveyer belt.

"Welcome aboard," Tapan says. Her luggage moves through the x-ray machine. Tapan watches the screen. He sees tiny sequined dresses, skimpy bikinis, forty or so different bottles of finger-nail polish, and a tangle of high heels.

"Do you have any water?" Bianchi says with a flirtatious smile. She looks away, giving him an opportunity to get hopelessly lost for a moment in her cleavage.

"We do not have any water. Do you have your ship ID?"

"It's right here I think," Bianchi says and digs around in her purse. "I just feel a little lightheaded. I could really use some water." She purses her lips and gives Tapan her best puppy-dog eyes.

Daniel glances at Bartek.

"Okay," Daniel says. "Now."

Bartek sets his duffel bags onto the belt and moves towards Vijay behind the kiosk. Daniel walks up the gangway and stops just before the entrance to the ship.

"Patryk," Daniel says. "Now."

Patryk walks up the gangway and stands close behind Daniel, out of sight of Tapan and Vijay. Bartek hands Vijay his ship ID card. The security guard pushes it into the slot on the front of the kiosk. *Bing!*

"Welcome aboard Mr…" Vijay says and looks down at a screen on the back of the kiosk. "Mr. Berlinski."

"Now," Daniel says softly. Bianchi lets out a cute little whimper, stumbles to her left toward the conveyor belt, and then collapses. Tapan and Vijay run towards her.

What happens in the next few seconds is like a perfectly synchronized ballet, one relentlessly rehearsed and now masterfully executed. Patryk slides past Daniel and bumps into Bartek. Bartek passes his ship ID to his twin and then slips past the gangway and onto the cruise ship. Bartek walks into the passenger stairwell. He's on deck 1. Midship. Elevators to his left. A staircase to his right. He walks up the staircase, the carpet a design of repeating starfish and chocolate melting cakes. He climbs four flights of stairs, reaches deck 5, and then walks into a men's restroom at the top of the stairway. He knew it would be here. They meticulously studied the cruise ship's deck plan. He locks himself in a stall and begins singing, as if to himself, the lyrics to Frank Sinatra's "The Way You Look Tonight." "Someday, when I'm awfully low."

"Bravo," Daniel says. Tapan and Vijay help Bianchi up.

"I am so sorry," Bianchi says adjusting her shirt. She's blushing, but it's fake. "I guess Señor Toads isn't the best way to start a cruise. I think I'm fine now."

"Are you sure?" Tapan says.

"Yes." She wipes her forehead. "I just need a few hours by the pool with a piña colada and I'll be back to normal. Thanks fellas. You two are the sweetest." She smiles, brushes herself off, takes her bag off the belt, and walks toward the kiosk. Vijay takes her ship ID card and slides it into the kiosk. *Bing!* She walks onto the cruise ship and takes an elevator up to her ocean-view suite on deck 10. The suite was just one of her many demands. An open bar tab was another. She won't get to enjoy either just yet. She needs to drop off her bag and then come back down to deck 6. Her job's not done for today.

Tapan and Vijay turn to Patryk.

"Have we checked you in?" Vijay says and walks over to the kiosk. Vijay looks down at the screen. Bartek's image is still there. "You can go. Welcome aboard Mr. Berlinski. How do you feel?"

"I'm feeling a little faint," Patryk says and puts a hand on his forehead. Vijay laughs. But Daniel isn't smiling. They have a long way to go and a very short amount of time to get this done. Tapan watches the screen as Patryk's duffel bags move through the x-ray machine. Tapan pushes a button. The belt stops. He pushes another button and the conveyor belt backs up a few inches.

"Wait just a minute," Tapan says, his eyes fixed to the x-ray screen. "I need you to open these bags." Tapan pushes a button. Patryk's bags emerge from the x-ray machine. "Open this one and empty the contents," Tapan says.

Patryk pulls out a wetsuit and then five small metal canisters, each small enough to fit in the palm of your hand.

"What are these?" Tapan says.

"They're back-up air canisters. Each one delivers about fifty breaths."

"Keep going," Tapan says.

Patryk pulls out a diving mask, a regulator, and an assortment of other diving gear. Then he pulls out a system of black straps that looks like a harness. Attached to the straps are two propellers the size of 2-liter bottles.

"This," Tapan says. "What is this?"

"It's a diving propulsion system called Jetboots. These propellers attach to each leg. It can propel a diver up to five miles per hour. This is the battery pack," Patryk says and points to a small black box dangling from a waist strap. Then he points to another small box with a few buttons on top. "This controls speed."

"Planning on diving?" Tapan says.

"Yeah, I'm diving the *Kennedy* off St. Thomas. I can swim fast with one of these babies."

"Looks fun," Tapan says. "Okay, go ahead."

Patryk throws the diving gear back in his duffle, grabs his other bag filled with clothes, and walks onto the ship. He climbs the staircase to deck 5 and enters the men's restroom.

Daniel is next. He places his leather suitcase on the conveyor belt. Tapan briefly inspects his bag and then Vijay slides his ship ID card into the kiosk. *Bing!*

"Welcome aboard Mr. Fuhrman. You're the last passenger to board today. I hope you enjoy your cruise."

"I think I will. Very much," Daniel says. He walks onto the ship. "Bravo," he says. Now Daniel smiles as he walks to the elevators and pushes the call button. He hears the security guards pull the gangway onto the ship. The elevator doors open. Inside is a couple wearing matching tropical shirts that read, "IT'S 5 O'CLOCK RIGHT HERE" across the front. They're holding drinks the size of fishbowls.

"Hey," the husband says, "does this elevator go to the front of the ship?"

His wife chuckles. Daniel pushes the button to close the elevator. As the glass doors close, the wife's smile fades, and the couple is sucked up toward the Lido Deck. Another elevator arrives. This one's empty, which is exactly what he needs. Elevators are one of the few places on cruise ships without cameras.

"Entering elevator," Daniel says. The door closes. He pushes the button for deck 5, then unzips his bag and pulls out a blue one-piece jumpsuit. It's identical to the jumpsuits worn by crewmembers on the "blue team," a group of deckhands that do everything from paint the ship to scrub the decks.

Bartek continues singing his Frank Sinatra tune. "Yes you're lovely, with your smile so warm."

Patryk, who is in the stall next to him, opens the duffle bag and pulls out a black uniform shirt with an embroidered patch across the arm that reads, "US CUSTOMS." He slides on the shirt, a pair of black pants, and a hat with the same patch on the front. Patryk pulls out a black backpack from the duffel bag and fills the pack with dive gear, then slides the duffel bag to Bartek in the next stall over. Bartek removes a blue jumpsuit, identical to Daniel's, from the duffel bag and pulls it over his clothes.

"Headed aft," Patryk says and steps out of the stall. He looks in the mirror as he walks out of the restroom. The US Customs uniform is a perfect match. He walks along the promenade toward the back of the ship, passing shops and cafés along the way. Patryk looks out the porthole windows along the promenade. He hears the ship's thrusters roar. The ship vibrates. He sees the concrete pier in Nassau drift away. The ship's horn is blasted. The deep thundering sound sends a surge of adrenaline through his body.

Bartek hears the horn blast and leaves the restroom. He's wearing the blue jumpsuit with a hat pulled low and a hip pack around his waist. He drops the duffel bags beside the restroom door. Bianchi is waiting by the elevators. She grabs the bags and takes the elevator to her stateroom. Now she's done. She'll go straight to the poolside bar. She already spotted a hot Italian officer she hopes will be there sunning in a speedo.

Bartek takes an elevator to deck 5. Daniel is there waiting. The ship is quiet. Most of the passengers are at the buffet enjoying their fourth meal of the day.

"Rendezvous," Daniel says.

Daniel and Bartek keep their heads down as they walk down the promenade toward the back of the ship. They stop about fifty feet from The Kitty Kat Lounge. In the evening, the lounge hosts karaoke and b-list singers. During the day, it's where the art auctions are held.

"Lounge," Daniel says.

Bartek and Daniel open a door marked, "CREW ONLY." It's a different world behind that door. All the colorful carpet, polished wood floors, and sparkling chandeliers disappear. They are standing in a long hallway lined with crew cabin doors, and everything is the same color, a dull tan. Two Filipino room stewards walk past Bartek and Daniel. One of the room stewards is talking about what type of noodles from the crew store he prefers.

"Prawn-lime. You find no better on ship. Trust me," he says and then starts singing the chorus to Brittany Spears' "Circus."

"Okay, what are we looking for?" Bartek says.

"These wires here," Daniel says and points to a bundle of cables that run the length of the hallway ceiling. "In the passenger area, all of these are neatly tucked away. They don't spend the money to hide them in crew areas. We just have to find the router box." They follow the bundle of wires to a small white box with several cables connected to it.

"That's it," Daniel says and points to the router. "Do your magic."

Bartek opens his hip pack and pulls out a small device with a 3-by-3-inch screen. Crew members are passing them as they work, but to the crew they're just two more guys from the blue team working on the ship. Even someone from the IT department wouldn't be suspicious. Contractors are always brought on board to work on special projects, and with more than 1,000 crew members working aboard the *Star of the Seas*, a new face in the crew area isn't unusual to see. It's as unremarkable as finding a musician in the crew bar at noon or day-old food in the crew mess.

Bartek connects a short black cable to his device and lifts the device up to the router. He points to a thin blue cable that's connected to the router. "This is the Cat6 Ethernet cable for Internet," he says and then points to a white cable that's also connected to the router. "This is the 1080p used for the camera feed. You ready?"

Daniel grabs the white video cable that's connected to the router. "Yeah."

"On three," Bartek says. "One, Two, Three." Daniel unplugs the white video cable from the router and plugs it into Bartek's device. Simultaneously, Bartek plugs the black cable from the device into the router.

Two decks below them a video surveillance team is sitting in a small tan room. If, at that moment, they had been watching the screen that displays the camera feed from the Kitty Kat Lounge, they would have seen a short flash of static. However, at that moment, the security nerds were watching the video feed from The Paris Theater where the dancers were rehearsing a section of their new production show called *Brazilian Carnival* that required all of the female dancers to wear tiny thongs. The video feed from The Kitty Kat Lounge could have turned off for an entire minute and the nerds wouldn't have noticed. The cruise ship could have violently listed from a rogue wave and the nerds would have died with their eyes glued to the image of seven cruise ship dancers hypnotically shaking their bums. At least they would have died happy.

The screen on Bartek's device lights up. Bartek can see the feed from the security camera in The Kitty Kat Lounge on one half of the screen and the video feed from an outdoor camera, the one behind the lounge that looks over the ship's rail at the back of the ship, on the other half of the screen. In the lounge, Bartek can see a red curtain that runs the length of the stage, and standing in front of the stage is a security guard hired by Art on the Ocean, the vendor that runs the art auctions on the cruise ship.

"They picked the wrong day to be frugal. One guard?" Daniel says.

Bartek presses a small button at the bottom of the screen, and the button lights up red.

"Recording," Daniel says. He looks at his watch. It will take about four minutes to complete the heist, but they only record one minute of video feed. Bartek hits the button again. The device stops recording and automatically plays the recorded footage from the two

Joshua Kinser

cameras on a loop.

Patryk is waiting on the breezeway of deck 5 starboard, watching Nassau slip away into the distance. He hears Daniel's voice in his earpiece. "Showtime."

Patryk walks to a side entrance. The glass doors slide open. He's engulfed by cold air as he enters the ship. He opens the door to The Kitty Kat Lounge. The security guard is startled when Patryk, a U.S. Customs official, walks into the lounge.

"Hi there," Patryk says and reads the guard's name tag, KENDRICK HOLDER, SECURITY, USA.

"Is there a problem?" Holder says.

"Mr. Kendrick Holder?" Patryk says.

"Yes." Holder's cheeks flush red.

"We're on board conducting an inspection," Patryk says. "There's an issue with your onboard paperwork. We don't have your complete medical records. We need you to go see Chief Security."

"Look, I'm not—"

"You must report to Chief Security," Patryk says "We don't have your medicals. That means you're on this ship illegally. I've been sent here to cover your position. You don't have a choice. We're very busy Mr. Holder. We have an entire ship to inspect. Now, if you will, please." Patryk gestures toward the door. "It will only take a few minutes. Then we can all move on with our day."

"Sorry. I understand," Holder says. He walks toward the door and then turns around. "Forward? Deck 1?"

"Excuse me?" Patryk says.

"Chief Security's office is forward, deck 1, right?"

"Oh, um, yes."

Mr. Holder turns around and walks out the door. Patryk begins to sweat.

"Four minutes," Patryk says.

"Counting," Daniel says.

Daniel calculated that it would take the security guard about seven minutes to walk to Chief Security's office at the front of the ship. Chief Security will run as fast as he can back to the lounge. He might even sound an alarm. But it doesn't matter. Patryk will be gone by then.

Patryk slips behind the curtain and into darkness. He reaches into his pocket and pulls out a small flashlight, twists it on, and points it toward the center of the stage, illuminating a portrait on a gold-painted easel. The painting is large, nearly 4-by-4-feet, and its wooden frame is intricately carved with tangles of spiraling roses and thorny stems. Carved in each corner is an inverted hand with the thumb and pinky finger curved outward. An eye, open wide and watching, is carved in the center of each palm.

Patryk points the light onto the painting's canvas. A woman is looking toward the sky with a long, thin outstretched neck. A golden shawl is draped across her shoulders. At her feet the shawl dissolves into a chaotic collage of red and black squares that become smaller and smaller, more and more pixelated as Patryk examines the length of the painting. She has a sublime, transcendent smile and dark hair that looks as if it's being blown around the canvas by a strong wind that sends black waves of hair flowing above her face. An abstract mosaic of expertly-laid gold leaf surrounds her and captures the motion of the spinning wind that engulfs the golden lady. This wind swirls around her, embraces her, like a shifting, ethereal squall. Patryk is speechless. Breathless. It is the Klimt.

"Executing," Patryk says.

"Yes," Daniel says. "We'll see you on shore. Good luck." Daniel starts a stopwatch. They will wait three more minutes before disconnecting Bartek's device from the video feed. The second blip of static will go unnoticed in the nerds' viewing room.

Patryk lays his backpack on the floor beneath the painting. He unzips the bag and removes the diving gear, a black wetsuit, and a black waterproof bag with shoulder straps. He takes off his shoes and hat and throws them into his backpack, and then carefully slides the painting into the waterproof bag. Before sealing the painting inside, he uses a small battery-powered pump to quickly remove any pockets of air. He pulls the wetsuit over his clothes. The Jetboots propulsion system is latched onto his legs. He grabs one of the back-up air canisters and throws the rest into the wetsuit's pockets. He slides the backpack and the waterproof bag containing the painting onto his back. The straps are cinched tight.

He walks out a door in the back of the stage and into a dressing room with a rack of costumes and a mirror surrounded by large, white bulbs. Next to the mirror is a door. Patryk cracks open the door and quickly peeks outside. The ship's railing at the back of the ship is in front of him. The ship's wide wake cuts a path all the way back to Nassau. He looks both directions down the breezeway. It's clear. He opens the door, walks across the breezeway, grabs the ship rails, and jumps overboard.

Five decks go by fast when you're freefalling. First he hears the thundering roar of the thrusters. Then he feels the sting of the water on his feet as he hits the surface of the ocean. Everything is quiet. A violent torrent of water pushes him away from the ship. He points his hands forward and is driven through the sea. He flips on the propulsion system and glides effortlessly through an endless blue.

Daniel and Bartek walk out of a restroom in the crew area that's next to the crew bar. They're back in their passenger clothes. The blue jumpsuits are stuffed in trashcans. They walk toward the door that leads into the passenger area. Daniel is reaching for the door handle when the door swings open and two crewmembers walk toward him. On the right is a Filipino room steward who's wearing a greyish-pink housekeeping uniform and a nametag that reads: BAYANI PINAGPALA, ROOM STEWARD, PHILIPPINES. To the left is a young man in a black suit with a black clip-on bowtie. His nametag reads: VLADIMIR NOVIKOV, CASINO, RUSSIA.

Vladimir looks at Daniel and Bartek. "Passengers are not allowed in crew areas."

"We got lost. Sorry," Daniel says and walks through

the door into the passenger area. As the door closes, Daniel can hear the Filipino ask the Russian, "How did you know they were passengers?"

"You're new," Vlad says. "You'll get the hang of it. Passengers are easy to spot. One, they smell good. Two, they have this strange healthy glow about them. And three, they don't look dog-ass tired."

"Oh," Beni says.

Patryk is cruising at nearly five miles per hour through the Atlantic. He's heading toward Nassau. It's easy to stay on track. He just follows the wake of the ship. He pushes a button on his watch. This sends his GPS coordinates to Billy McMathews, who's racing toward the cruise ship in a small inflatable dinghy. Patryk's coordinates appear on the screen of Billy's GPS unit. He drives the boat to a spot about fifteen-hundred feet from the ship and then kills the motor. Patryk pops out of the ocean and pulls the mask off his face.

"Let the fucking celebrations begin, old sport," Billy says, with a cigarette dangling from his lips, as he pulls Patryk onto the dinghy.

"That was intense," Patryk says as rips the propulsion gear from his legs.

"It's not over yet buddy," Billy says. "Not until we're drinking Jamison on the rocks, rolling dice with a pair of red-headed Irish girls, and riding fucking dolphins in Atlantis. Hold on!" Billy cranks the motor, whips the boat around, and speeds off toward Nassau.

Daniel and Bartek split up immediately. As Daniel rides the elevator to deck 12, he lets out a deep breath. He is slowly returning to reality. While the heist was happening, Daniel was in the zone. His adrenaline was running at full speed. He was inside of a focused tunnel. No sound. No feeling.

Now he can feel his heart pounding in his chest, his pulse hammering up his neck. Now he can hear the roar of the engine as he walks to his stateroom at the end of the hall. He shoves in his keycard and opens the door.

Soft jazz is playing from the bedside radio. He walks to the mini bar and pours a shot of Cognac over a few square cubes of ice, and then collapses into the plush comfort of a leather chair with a view that looks out across the choppy ocean. He sits there; completely still. The sea is churning. A heavy rain is falling from a leaden sky. White caps are breaking in the wind of the oncoming tropical storm. He looks over the skyline of Nassau and allows a wave of excitement and satisfaction to crawl across his body, his mind, his spirit.

Daniel opens the suitcase that Bianchi delivered to the room. He pulls out his Bible, flips the book open to a random page, and then reads the first verse that catches his eye. It's from Jeremiah, 17:11, *"Like a partridge that hatches eggs it did not lay are those who gain riches by unjust means. When their lives are half gone, their riches will desert them, and in the end they will prove to be fools."*

"So true," Daniel says. "So appropriate." But Daniel

deeply feels that there are still rough seas ahead, and this troubles him. He looks out toward the ocean and sinks into the chair. His body has finally relaxed. The adrenaline has worn off now and he feels extremely tired. The last thing he sees before falling asleep is Billy's inflatable dinghy bouncing across the whitecaps, racing toward Nassau, battling toward victory through a pelting rain.

Daniel is jolted awake. His phone is vibrating in his pocket. He glances at his watch. It's 6:14 p.m. More than three hours have passed since the heist. He looks at the number displayed on his phone. It's Patryk.

"This is Daniel," he says.

"Daniel," Patryk says. "Are you sitting down?"

"Yes. Why?"

"The painting is a fake. The Klimt is a fake."

"That's impossible. We tracked the painting for months. We followed it to the ship. We were positive this was the original. I don't believe it. Are you sure?" Daniel says. He knows this could be a heist on him. But why would Patryk do such a thing under the circumstances? It just wouldn't make sense.

"I wouldn't say it if I wasn't sure," Patryk says. "We've had our experts look at it. It's a fake, but it's an expert fake."

"What do you think we should do?" Daniel says. Maybe Patryk will reveal something in his answer.

"We should get off the ship and find the real Klimt." A pause.

"No," Daniel says. "We should stay on board."

"Why would you want to do that? You know what's at stake."

"I know exactly what's at stake," Daniel says. "We looked in the obvious place, but it wasn't the right place. I am certain the original came aboard in Miami. We have to stay on board. We have to stay on board, because the painting is still on this ship."

*****~~~~~*****

Other Books By Joshua Kinser:

The Cruise Ship Capers: An Art Heist on the High Seas.

Following Mowgli: An Appalachian Trail Adventure with the World's Most Hilarious Dog.

Hiking South Carolina: A Guide to the State's Greatest Hikes. Published by Falcon Guides.

Florida Gulf Coast, 3rd and 4th editions. Published by Moon Handbooks.

Five Star Trails: Raleigh and Durham: Your Guide to the Area's Most Beautiful Hikes. Published by Menasha Ridge Press.

Five Star Trails: Charlotte: Your Guide to the Area's Most Beautiful Hikes. Published by Menasha Ridge Press.

For a complete and up-to-date list of Joshua's books, visit his author page at Amazon.com.

Now that you've finished my book, will you please consider writing a review?

www.amazon.com/Chronicles-Answers-Questions-Passenger-ebook/dp/B007Q3LSYQ

Reviews are the best way for readers to discover great new books. I would truly appreciate it. And thank you for purchasing and reading my book.

ABOUT THE AUTHOR

Joshua Kinser is author of *Chronicles of a Cruise Ship Crew Member*, a comical memoir about what it's really like to work on a cruise ship, which has been a #1 bestseller in Amazon's "Cruise" and "Caribbean" categories. For his cruise ship series books, he draws from his experiences working as a musician and as an art director aboard cruise ships for more than six years. He is the author of five internationally distributed travel guides including *Florida Gulf Coast* published by Moon Handbooks and *Hiking South Carolina* published by Falcon Guides. He has worked as a staff writer for Gannett with the *Pensacola News Journal* and has published articles in magazines such as *SAIL*, *Dance Spirit*, and *Times of the Islands*. He has written over 200 articles online for websites such as Trails.com and USA Today Travel. He currently splits his time between Black Mountain, North Carolina and Gulf Breeze, Florida.

Feel free to contact him at: **Joshuakinser@gmail.com**